EYEWITNESS VISUAL DICTIONARIES

THE VISUAL DICTIONARY *of the*
HORSE

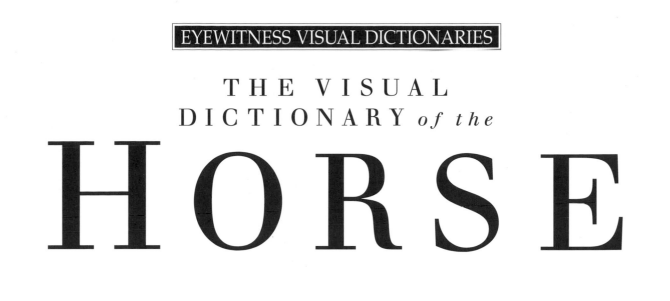

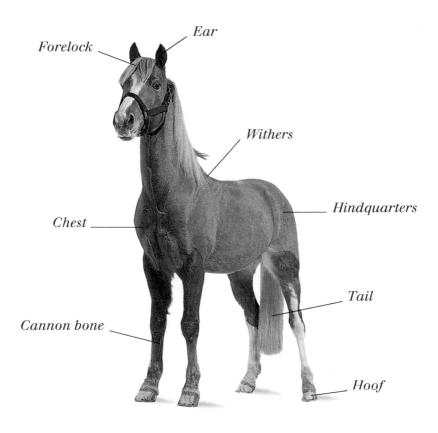

Forelock · Ear · Withers · Chest · Hindquarters · Cannon bone · Tail · Hoof

**EXTERNAL FEATURES
OF A HORSE**

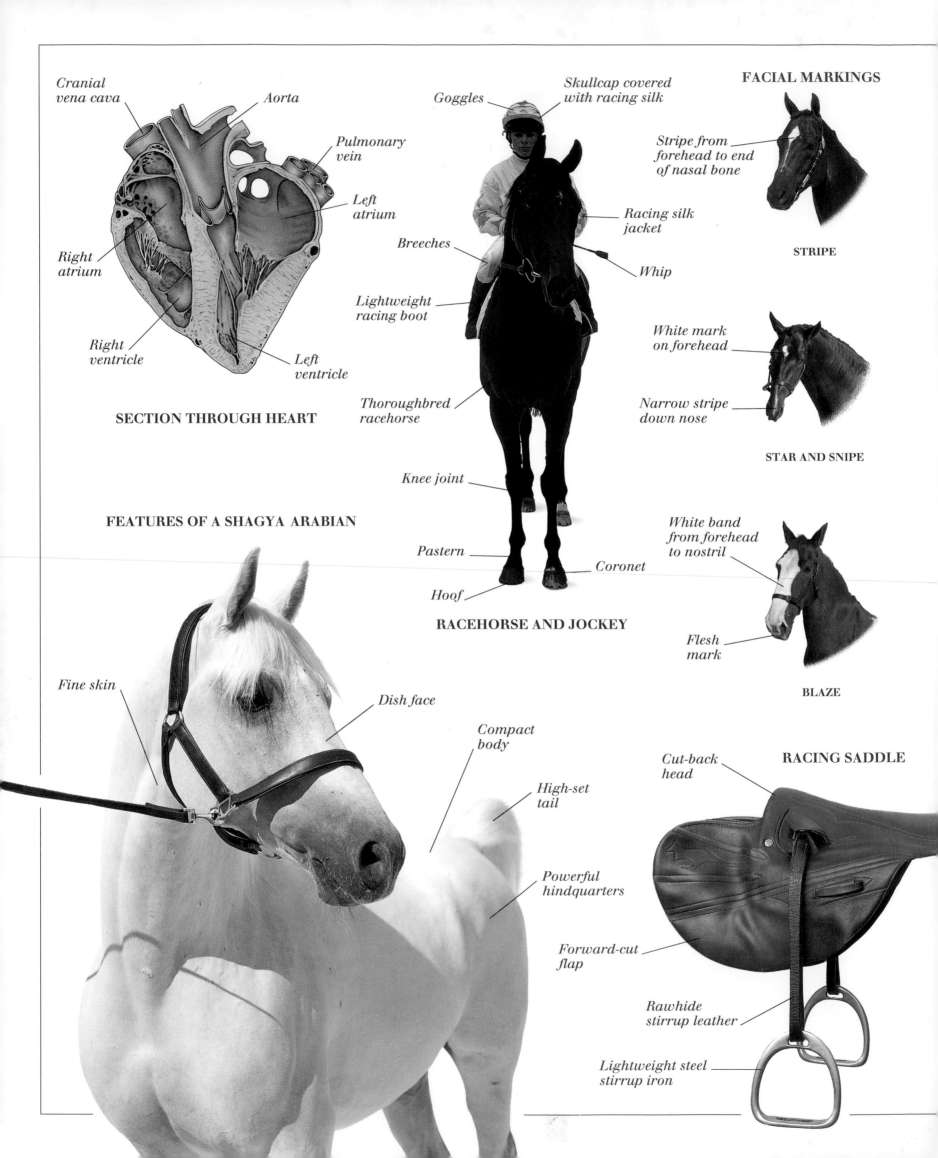

SECTION THROUGH HEART

Cranial vena cava
Aorta
Pulmonary vein
Left atrium
Right atrium
Right ventricle
Left ventricle

FEATURES OF A SHAGYA ARABIAN

Fine skin
Dish face
Compact body
High-set tail
Powerful hindquarters

RACEHORSE AND JOCKEY

Goggles
Skullcap covered with racing silk
Racing silk jacket
Breeches
Whip
Lightweight racing boot
Thoroughbred racehorse
Knee joint
Pastern
Hoof
Coronet

FACIAL MARKINGS

Stripe from forehead to end of nasal bone

STRIPE

White mark on forehead
Narrow stripe down nose

STAR AND SNIPE

White band from forehead to nostril
Flesh mark

BLAZE

RACING SADDLE

Cut-back head
Forward-cut flap
Rawhide stirrup leather
Lightweight steel stirrup iron

THE VISUAL
DICTIONARY *of the*
HORSE

Seat

Footrest

Afterwale

Collar

Saddle flap

Breeching strap

Wagon

Blinder

Bridle

Rein

Trace chain

Tug

Belly band

Shaft

Cantle

HORSE HARNESSED TO WAGON

DK

DORLING KINDERSLEY
LONDON • NEW YORK • STUTTGART

A DORLING KINDERSLEY BOOK

ART EDITOR PAUL CALVER
DESIGN ASSISTANT SUSAN KNIGHT

PROJECT EDITOR LOUISE TUCKER
CONSULTANT EDITORS DR. JULIET CLUTTON-BROCK, SARAH MORGAN
US EDITOR JILL HAMILTON
US CONSULTANT SHARON RALLS LEMON

MANAGING ART EDITOR PHILIP GILDERDALE
SENIOR EDITOR MARTYN PAGE
MANAGING EDITOR RUTH MIDGLEY

ILLUSTRATIONS DAN WRIGHT, TONY GRAHAM, JOANNA CAMERON
PRODUCTION JAYNE SIMPSON

Powerful neck

Broad, powerful chest

ARDENNAIS

Yellowish red coat

Black mane

LUSITANO

Powerful hindquarters

Straight profile

BRETON

Compact body

Well-defined withers

ANGLO-ARAB

Low withers

Small head

DARTMOOR PONY

EXAMPLES OF HORSE BREEDS

FIRST AMERICAN EDITION, 1994

2 4 6 8 10 9 7 5 3 1

PUBLISHED IN THE UNITED STATES BY
DORLING KINDERSLEY PUBLISHING, INC., 95 MADISON AVENUE
NEW YORK, NEW YORK 10016

LIBRARY OF CONGRESS CATALOGING-IN-PUBLICATION DATA

HORSE.
   p. cm. — (EYEWITNESS VISUAL DICTIONARIES)
        INCLUDES INDEX.

ISBN 1-56458-504-2
1. HORSES—TERMINOLOGY. 2. HORSES—PICTORIAL WORKS.
3. PICTURE DICTIONARIES, ENGLISH. I. SERIES.
SF278.H68 1993
636.1—dc20   93-20819
                                                    CIP
                                                    AC
REPRODUCED BY COLOURSCAN, SINGAPORE
PRINTED AND BOUND IN VERONA, ITALY, BY ARNOLDO MONDADORI

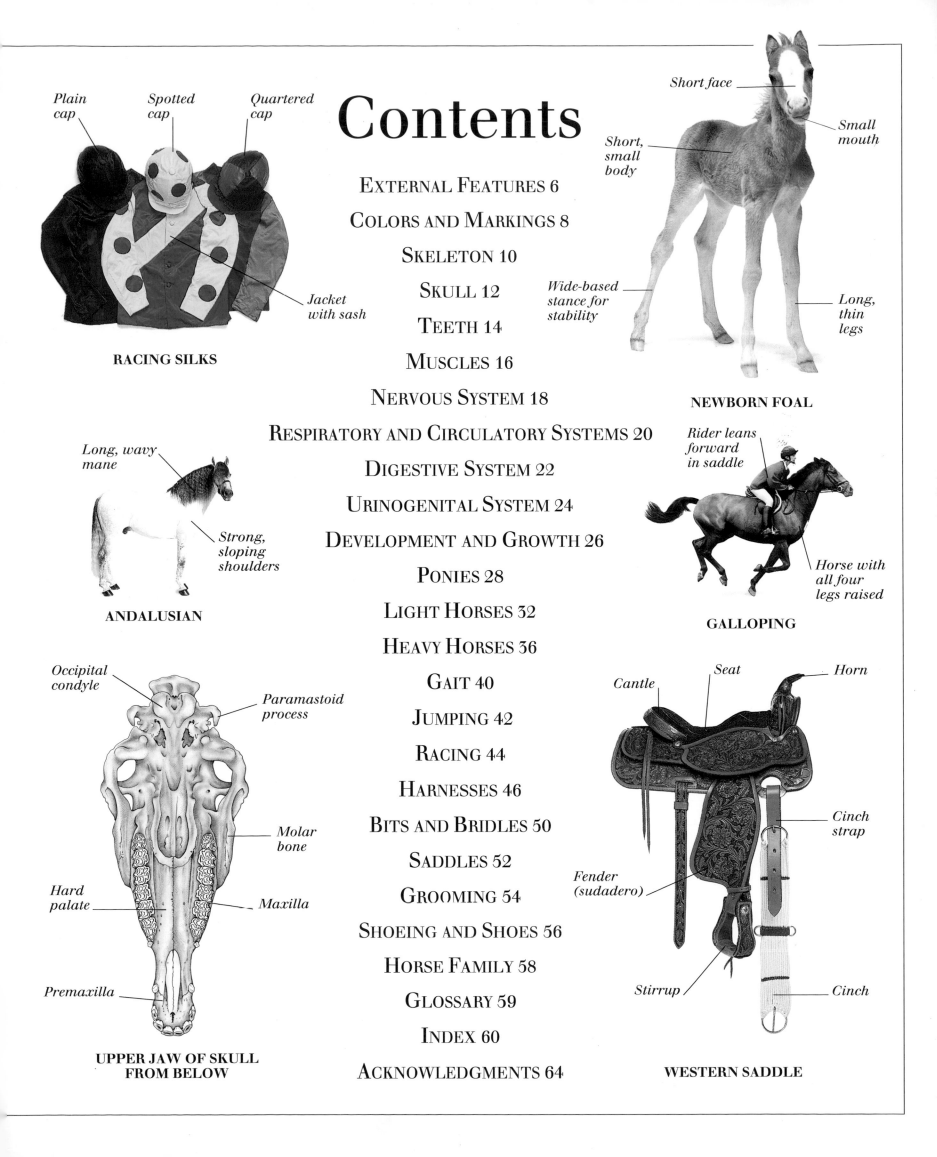

Plain cap

Spotted cap

Quartered cap

Jacket with sash

RACING SILKS

Long, wavy mane

Strong, sloping shoulders

ANDALUSIAN

Occipital condyle

Paramastoid process

Molar bone

Hard palate

Maxilla

Premaxilla

UPPER JAW OF SKULL FROM BELOW

Contents

EXTERNAL FEATURES 6

COLORS AND MARKINGS 8

SKELETON 10

SKULL 12

TEETH 14

MUSCLES 16

NERVOUS SYSTEM 18

RESPIRATORY AND CIRCULATORY SYSTEMS 20

DIGESTIVE SYSTEM 22

URINOGENITAL SYSTEM 24

DEVELOPMENT AND GROWTH 26

PONIES 28

LIGHT HORSES 32

HEAVY HORSES 36

GAIT 40

JUMPING 42

RACING 44

HARNESSES 46

BITS AND BRIDLES 50

SADDLES 52

GROOMING 54

SHOEING AND SHOES 56

HORSE FAMILY 58

GLOSSARY 59

INDEX 60

ACKNOWLEDGMENTS 64

Short face

Small mouth

Short, small body

Wide-based stance for stability

Long, thin legs

NEWBORN FOAL

Rider leans forward in saddle

Horse with all four legs raised

GALLOPING

Cantle

Seat

Horn

Cinch strap

Fender (sudadero)

Stirrup

Cinch

WESTERN SADDLE

External features

ALTHOUGH THE APPEARANCE OF MODERN HORSES varies enormously among breeds, all horses are descended from ancestral wild horses. The process of selective breeding over hundreds of years has led to the great variation among the many breeds. Most breeds of horse fall into one of three categories: ponies, light horses, or heavy horses. Breeds are divided into these categories by differences in weight, gait, color, body build and proportion, and height. A horse's height is the distance from the top of the horse's withers to the ground. It is traditionally measured in hands, based on the approximate width of a man's hand, four inches. Light horses are chiefly differentiated from heavy horses by body build and proportion. Ponies are usually differentiated from all other horses by height; ponies are less than 14.2 hands (58 in) high. Despite the differences between breeds, all horses have certain physical features in common, known as points. The points of a horse are the visible external features, such as the tail and the ear, as well as the parts of the skeleton and the superficial muscles that can be felt through the skin, such as the facial crest and jugular groove.

TYPES OF HORSE

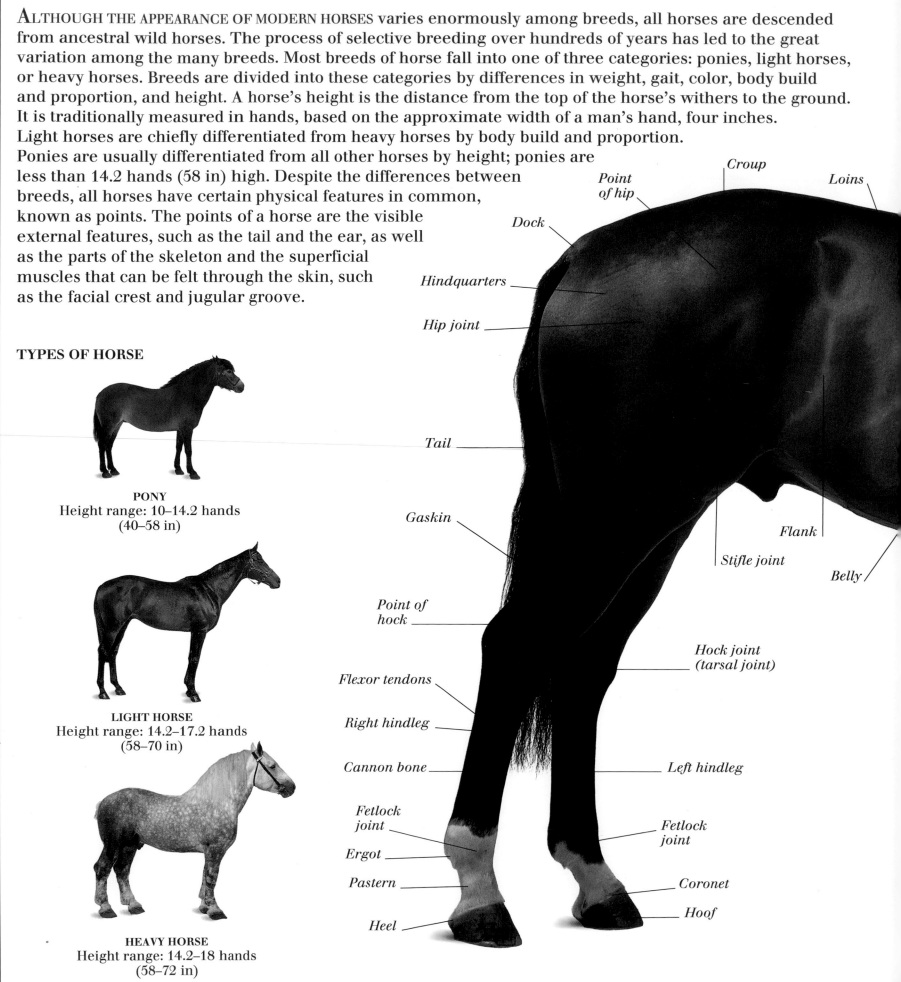

PONY
Height range: 10–14.2 hands
(40–58 in)

LIGHT HORSE
Height range: 14.2–17.2 hands
(58–70 in)

HEAVY HORSE
Height range: 14.2–18 hands
(58–72 in)

Croup

Point of hip

Loins

Dock

Hindquarters

Hip joint

Tail

Gaskin

Flank

Stifle joint

Belly

Point of hock

Hock joint
(tarsal joint)

Flexor tendons

Right hindleg

Cannon bone

Left hindleg

Fetlock joint

Fetlock joint

Ergot

Pastern

Coronet

Hoof

Heel

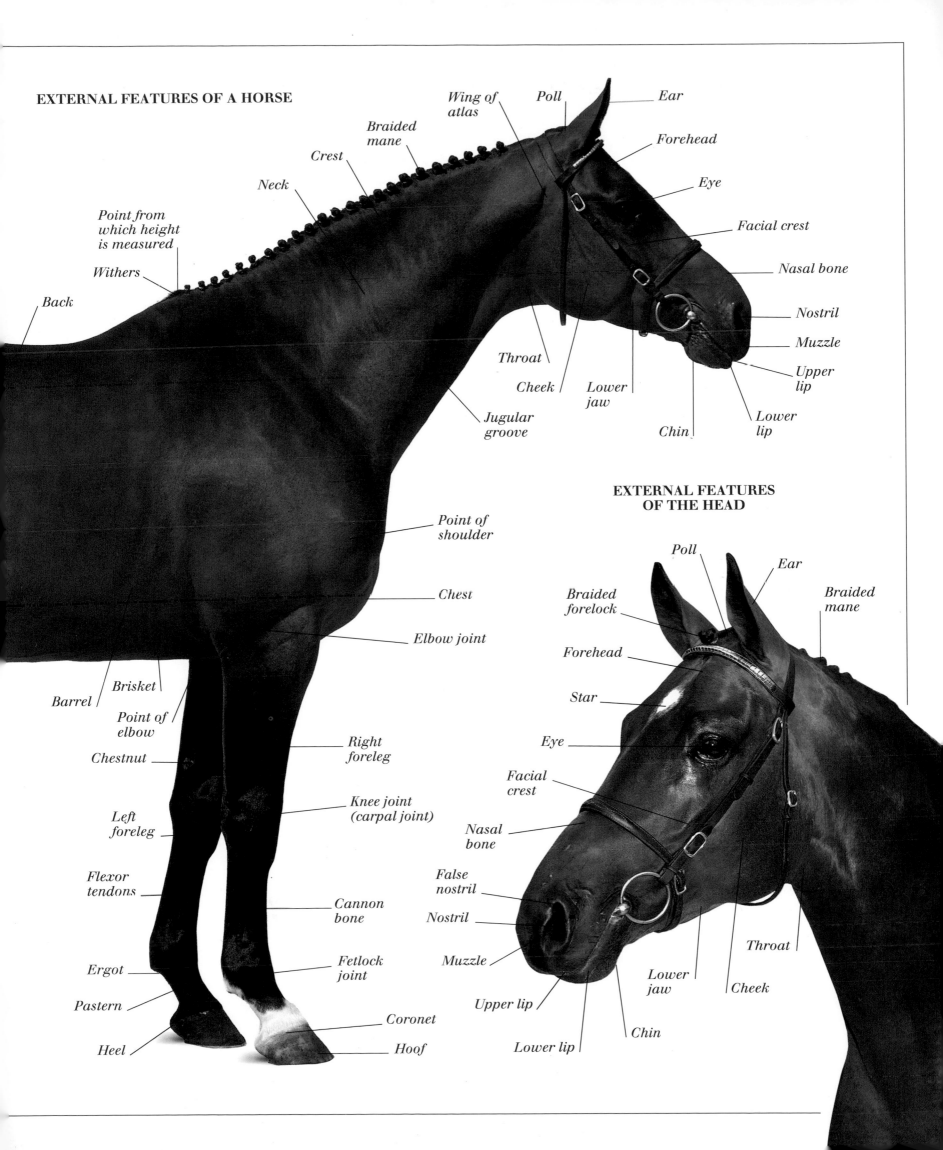

EXTERNAL FEATURES OF A HORSE

Wing of atlas

Poll

Ear

Braided mane

Forehead

Crest

Eye

Neck

Facial crest

Point from which height is measured

Nasal bone

Withers

Nostril

Back

Muzzle

Throat

Upper lip

Cheek

Lower jaw

Lower lip

Jugular groove

Chin

EXTERNAL FEATURES OF THE HEAD

Point of shoulder

Poll

Ear

Braided forelock

Braided mane

Chest

Forehead

Elbow joint

Star

Eye

Brisket

Facial crest

Barrel

Point of elbow

Right foreleg

Nasal bone

Chestnut

Knee joint (carpal joint)

False nostril

Left foreleg

Nostril

Flexor tendons

Throat

Cannon bone

Muzzle

Ergot

Fetlock joint

Lower jaw

Cheek

Pastern

Upper lip

Chin

Heel

Coronet

Lower lip

Hoof

Colors and markings

ALL PRESENT-DAY DOMESTIC HORSES are descended from dun-colored wild horses. Dun horses typically have a yellowish red or light reddish brown main coat with a dark mane and tail. Today, selective breeding has produced a range of colors, such as bay, chestnut, and gray. Most are defined by the coat alone, although some are distinguished by a combination of the coat color with specific mane and tail colors. For example, a Palomino horse has a gold coat with a white mane and tail. Some breeds are selectively bred to be one particular color, so the Friesian horse is always black. Combinations of colors on the coat also have special terms, so a dapple gray coat has small dark gray rings on a paler gray base. The white markings on the face and legs have particular names. For example, a white patch on the forehead is known as a star, and white hair reaching up to the knee or hock is called a stocking.

FACIAL MARKINGS

STAR   STRIPE

BLAZE   BALD FACE

STAR AND SNIPE   SNIPE

PONY WITH
DORSAL STRIPE

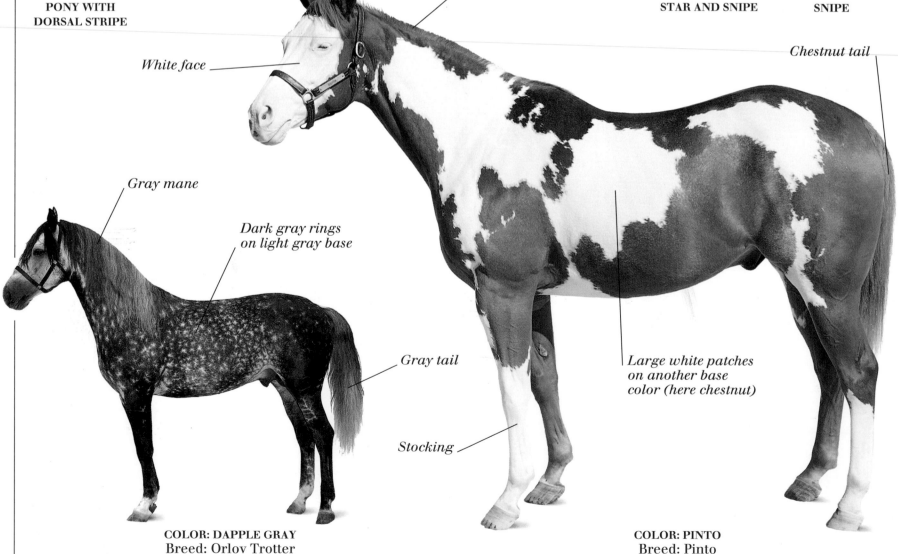

Chestnut mane

White face

Chestnut tail

Gray mane

*Dark gray rings
on light gray base*

Gray tail

*Large white patches
on another base
color (here chestnut)*

Stocking

COLOR: DAPPLE GRAY
Breed: Orlov Trotter

COLOR: PINTO
Breed: Pinto

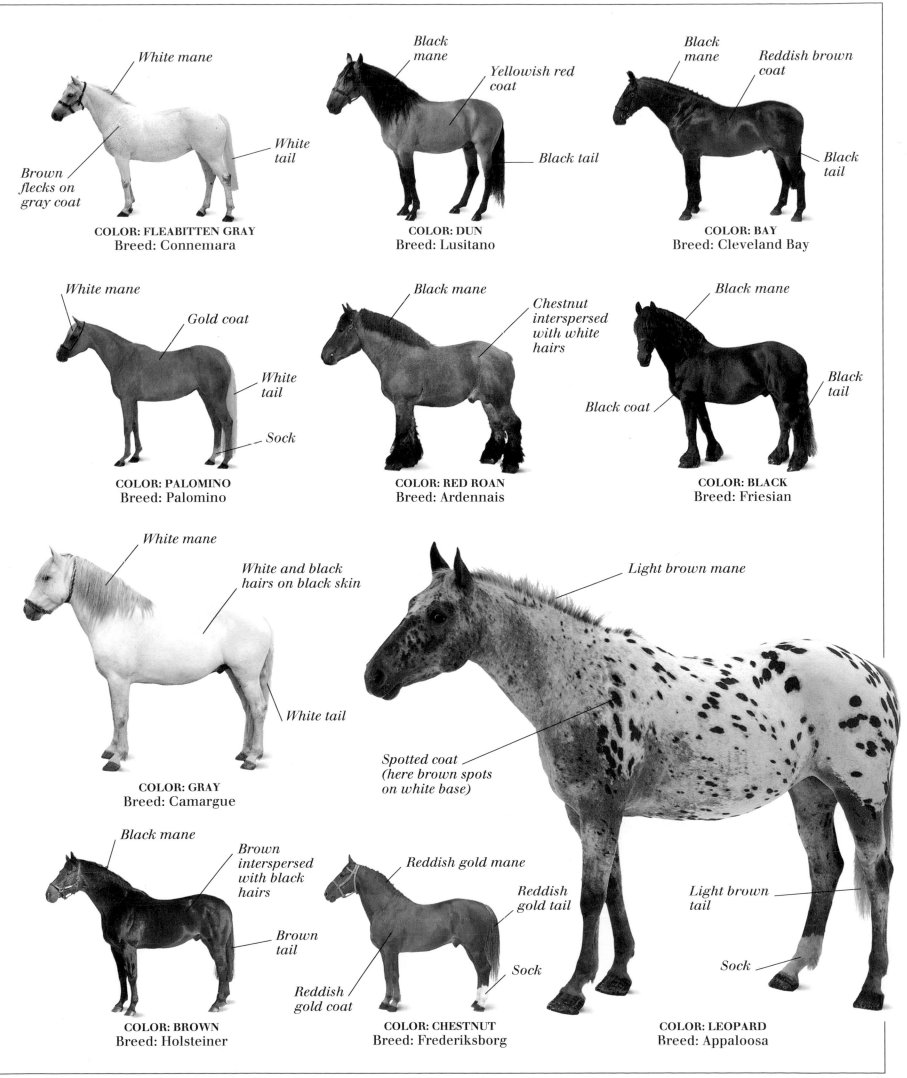

White mane

Brown flecks on gray coat

White tail

COLOR: FLEABITTEN GRAY
Breed: Connemara

Black mane

Yellowish red coat

Black tail

COLOR: DUN
Breed: Lusitano

Black mane

Reddish brown coat

Black tail

COLOR: BAY
Breed: Cleveland Bay

White mane

Gold coat

White tail

Sock

COLOR: PALOMINO
Breed: Palomino

Black mane

Chestnut interspersed with white hairs

COLOR: RED ROAN
Breed: Ardennais

Black mane

Black coat

Black tail

COLOR: BLACK
Breed: Friesian

White mane

White and black hairs on black skin

White tail

COLOR: GRAY
Breed: Camargue

Light brown mane

Spotted coat (here brown spots on white base)

Light brown tail

Sock

COLOR: LEOPARD
Breed: Appaloosa

Black mane

Brown interspersed with black hairs

Brown tail

COLOR: BROWN
Breed: Holsteiner

Reddish gold mane

Reddish gold tail

Sock

Reddish gold coat

COLOR: CHESTNUT
Breed: Frederiksborg

Skeleton

THE HORSE'S SKELETON IS A STRONG but flexible framework, made up of about 205 bones, that supports and protects the soft tissues of the body. The spinal vertebrae form a column that helps the back support the weight of the body organs, and transmits the propelling force of the hindlegs to the rest of the body. Joints, such as the hock and stifle, give the legs flexibility and also act as shock absorbers. Each leg has only one digit (corresponding to the middle finger or toe of a human), which bears the horse's weight and is enclosed at the end by the hoof. In addition to supporting and protecting body organs, the skeleton has two other important functions. It stores the minerals calcium and phosphorus, and it helps produce red and white blood corpuscles.

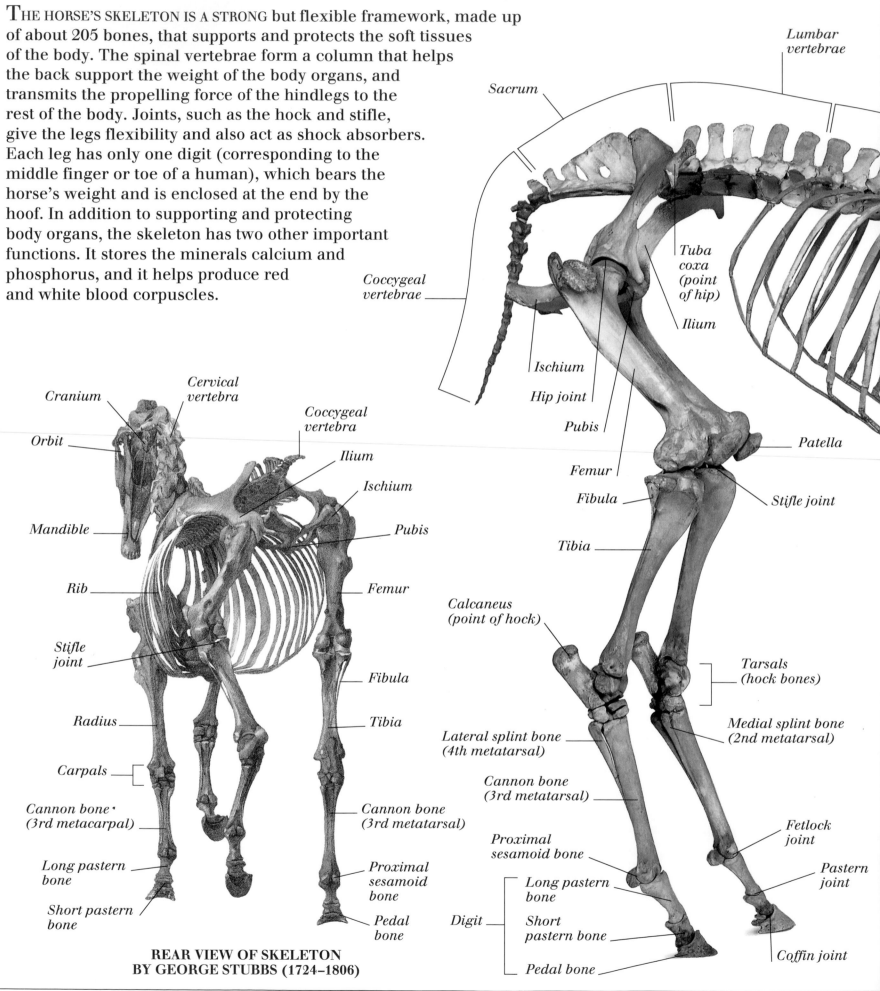

**REAR VIEW OF SKELETON
BY GEORGE STUBBS (1724–1806)**

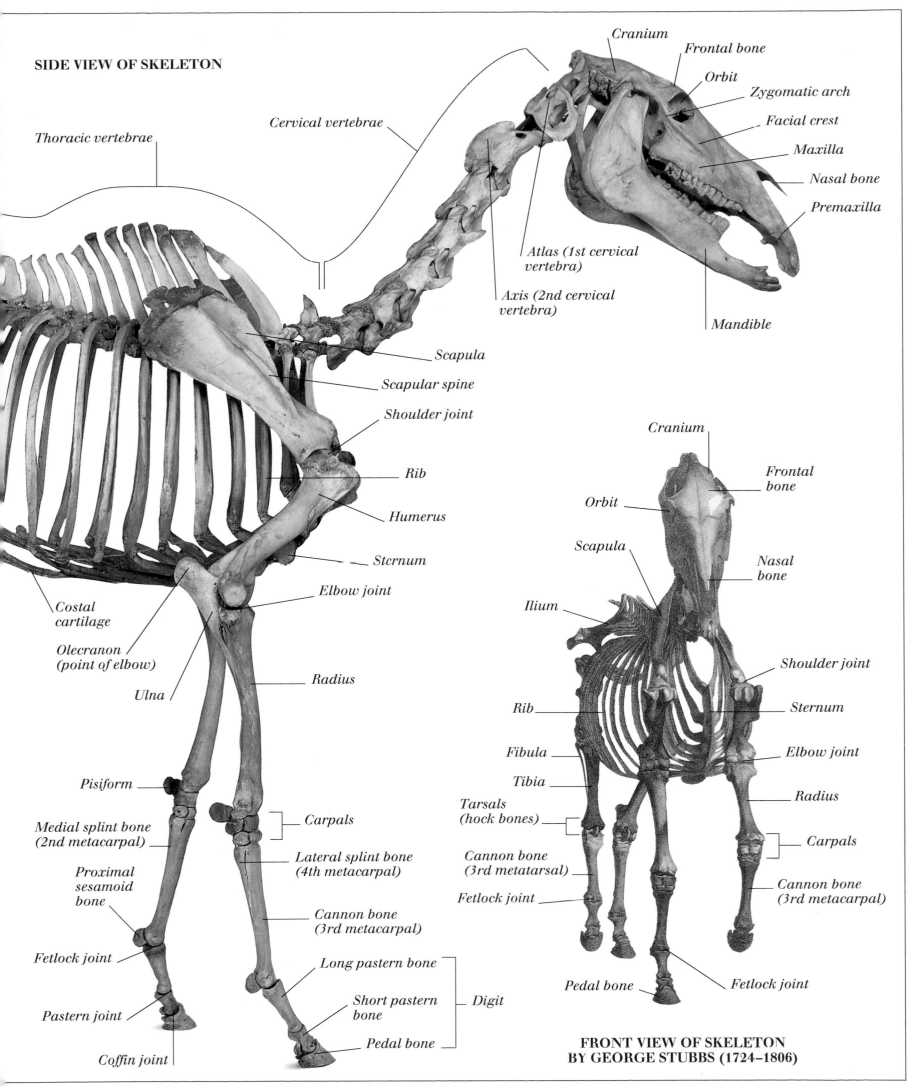

SIDE VIEW OF SKELETON

Thoracic vertebrae

Cervical vertebrae

Cranium

Frontal bone

Orbit

Zygomatic arch

Facial crest

Maxilla

Nasal bone

Premaxilla

Atlas (1st cervical vertebra)

Axis (2nd cervical vertebra)

Mandible

Scapula

Scapular spine

Shoulder joint

Rib

Humerus

Sternum

Elbow joint

Costal cartilage

Olecranon (point of elbow)

Radius

Ulna

Pisiform

Medial splint bone (2nd metacarpal)

Carpals

Lateral splint bone (4th metacarpal)

Proximal sesamoid bone

Cannon bone (3rd metacarpal)

Fetlock joint

Long pastern bone

Pastern joint

Short pastern bone

Digit

Coffin joint

Pedal bone

Cranium

Frontal bone

Orbit

Nasal bone

Scapula

Ilium

Shoulder joint

Rib

Sternum

Fibula

Elbow joint

Tibia

Radius

Tarsals (hock bones)

Carpals

Cannon bone (3rd metatarsal)

Cannon bone (3rd metacarpal)

Fetlock joint

Pedal bone

Fetlock joint

FRONT VIEW OF SKELETON BY GEORGE STUBBS (1724–1806)

Skull

**SKULL BY
GEORGE STUBBS
(1724–1806)**

THE SKULL IS MADE UP OF 34 bones (including the three small bones in each middle ear), most of which are fused together to form a strong, rigid structure that protects the brain and sensory organs of the head and holds the teeth. At the back of the skull, two bones (called occipital condyles) make a flexible joint with the cervical vertebrae (neck bones). Above the occipital condyles is the cranium, which surrounds the cranial cavity that houses the brain. The brain is connected to the spinal cord through a passage called the foramen magnum. There are several other foramina (passages) to allow nerves and blood vessels to pass into and out of the skull. At the front of the skull are the large orbits that house the eyes and the nasal bones that protect the nasal organs. Inside the skull there are spaces—called cavities if they contain organs, or sinuses if they contain only air. The largest bone of the skull is the mandible (lower jaw). Together with the maxilla and premaxilla (which form the upper jaw), the mandible holds the horse's teeth (see pp. 14-15).

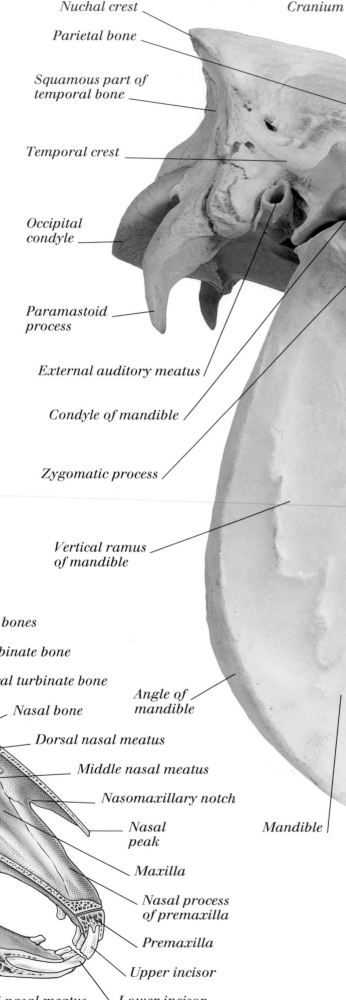

Nuchal crest
Cranium
Parietal bone
Squamous part of temporal bone
Temporal crest
Occipital condyle
Paramastoid process
External auditory meatus
Condyle of mandible
Zygomatic process
Vertical ramus of mandible
Angle of mandible
Mandible

SECTION THROUGH SKULL

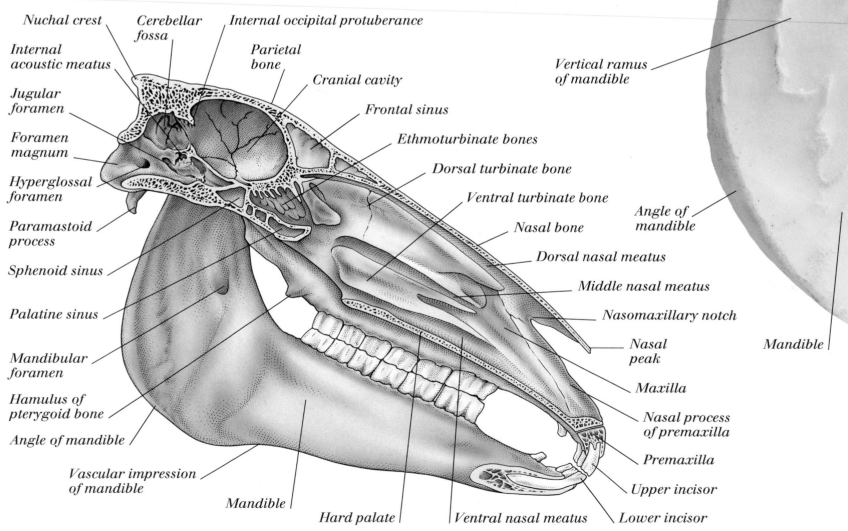

Nuchal crest
Cerebellar fossa
Internal occipital protuberance
Internal acoustic meatus
Parietal bone
Jugular foramen
Cranial cavity
Foramen magnum
Frontal sinus
Hyperglossal foramen
Ethmoturbinate bones
Paramastoid process
Dorsal turbinate bone
Sphenoid sinus
Ventral turbinate bone
Nasal bone
Palatine sinus
Dorsal nasal meatus
Middle nasal meatus
Mandibular foramen
Nasomaxillary notch
Hamulus of pterygoid bone
Nasal peak
Angle of mandible
Maxilla
Nasal process of premaxilla
Vascular impression of mandible
Premaxilla
Mandible
Upper incisor
Hard palate
Ventral nasal meatus
Lower incisor

12

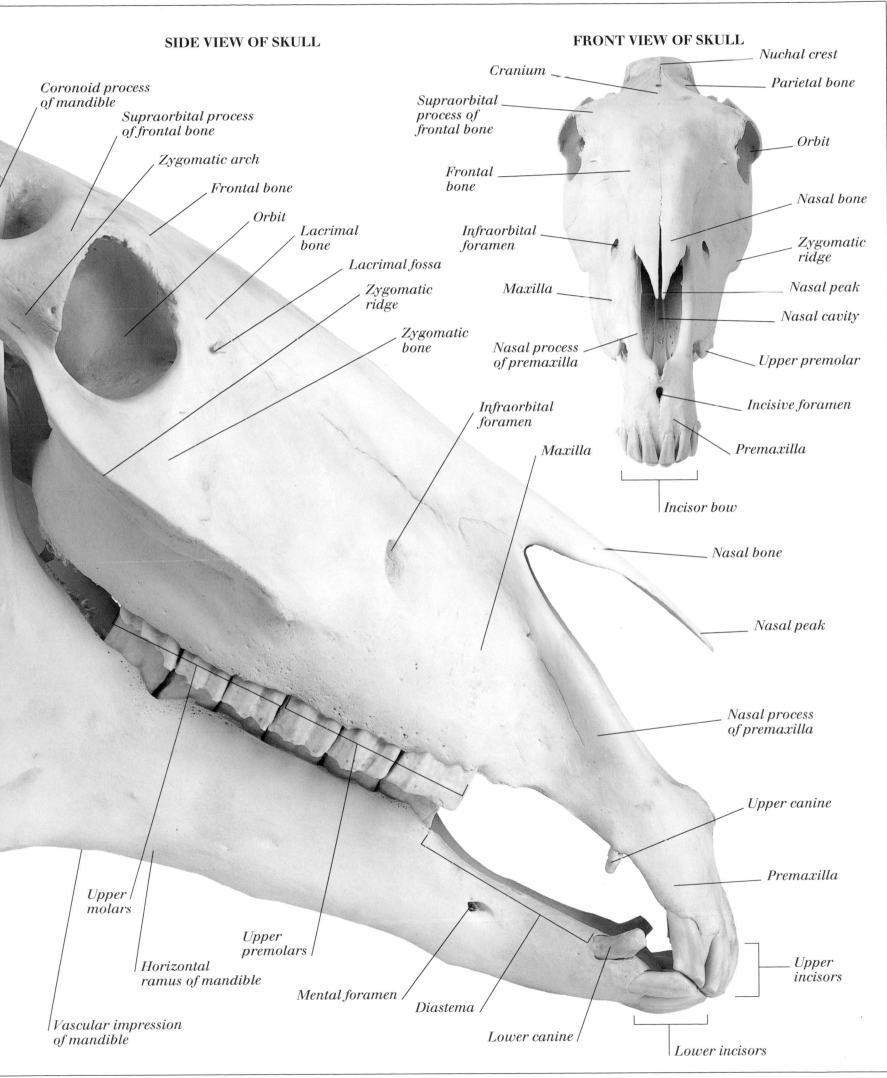

SIDE VIEW OF SKULL

Coronoid process
of mandible

Supraorbital process
of frontal bone

Zygomatic arch

Frontal bone

Orbit

Lacrimal
bone

Lacrimal fossa

Zygomatic
ridge

Zygomatic
bone

Infraorbital
foramen

Maxilla

Upper
molars

Upper
premolars

Horizontal
ramus of mandible

Mental foramen

Diastema

Lower canine

Vascular impression
of mandible

FRONT VIEW OF SKULL

Cranium

Nuchal crest

Parietal bone

Supraorbital
process of
frontal bone

Orbit

Frontal
bone

Nasal bone

Infraorbital
foramen

Zygomatic
ridge

Nasal peak

Maxilla

Nasal cavity

Nasal process
of premaxilla

Upper premolar

Incisive foramen

Premaxilla

Incisor bow

Nasal bone

Nasal peak

Nasal process
of premaxilla

Upper canine

Premaxilla

Upper
incisors

Lower incisors

13

Teeth

STRONG TEETH AND JAWS enable the horse to eat
its staple food of grass. The high-crowned teeth
are held in the powerful bone structures of the
premaxilla and maxilla (which together form
the upper jaw) and the mandible (lower jaw).
The foal has a set of milk teeth that wear down
as it begins to graze. Then the adult or permanent
teeth gradually replace the milk teeth, so that the
horse has a complete set of permanent teeth by
the time it is five years old. An adult horse usually
has 40 teeth—12 incisors, 4 canines, 12 premolars,
and 12 molars—although in the female the canines
may be small or absent. Permanent teeth have
short roots and long crowns when they first
erupt, but the crowns wear down as the horse
ages. Teeth are composed of vertical layers of
enamel, dentine, and cement that wear down
at different rates, leaving the surface uneven
and exposing different surface features. The age
of a horse can be estimated from the wear on its
teeth, particularly on the surface of the incisors,
and from the development of Galvayne's groove.

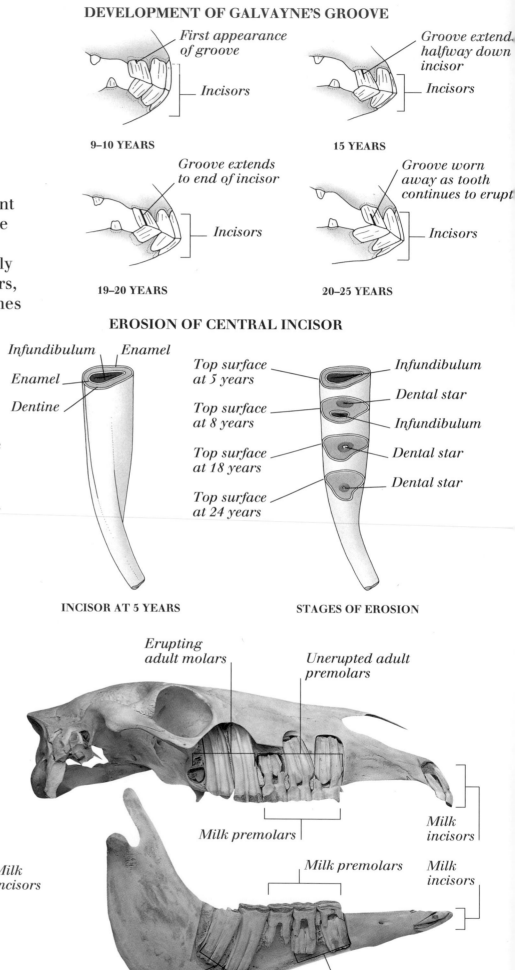

DEVELOPMENT OF GALVAYNE'S GROOVE

First appearance of groove

Incisors

9–10 YEARS

Groove extends halfway down incisor

Incisors

15 YEARS

Groove extends to end of incisor

Incisors

19–20 YEARS

Groove worn away as tooth continues to erupt

Incisors

20–25 YEARS

EROSION OF CENTRAL INCISOR

Infundibulum   Enamel

Enamel

Dentine

Top surface at 5 years

Top surface at 8 years

Top surface at 18 years

Top surface at 24 years

Infundibulum

Dental star

Infundibulum

Dental star

Dental star

INCISOR AT 5 YEARS

STAGES OF EROSION

DEVELOPMENT OF TEETH

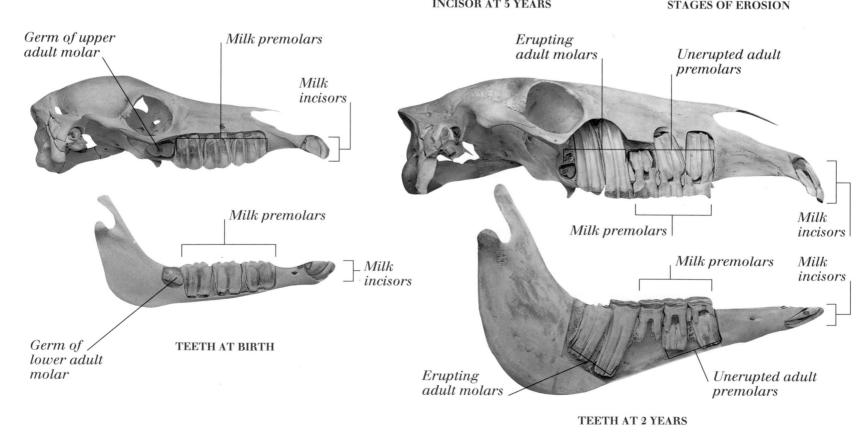

Germ of upper adult molar

Milk premolars

Milk incisors

Milk premolars

Milk incisors

Germ of lower adult molar

TEETH AT BIRTH

Erupting adult molars

Unerupted adult premolars

Milk premolars

Milk incisors

Milk premolars

Milk incisors

Erupting adult molars

Unerupted adult premolars

TEETH AT 2 YEARS

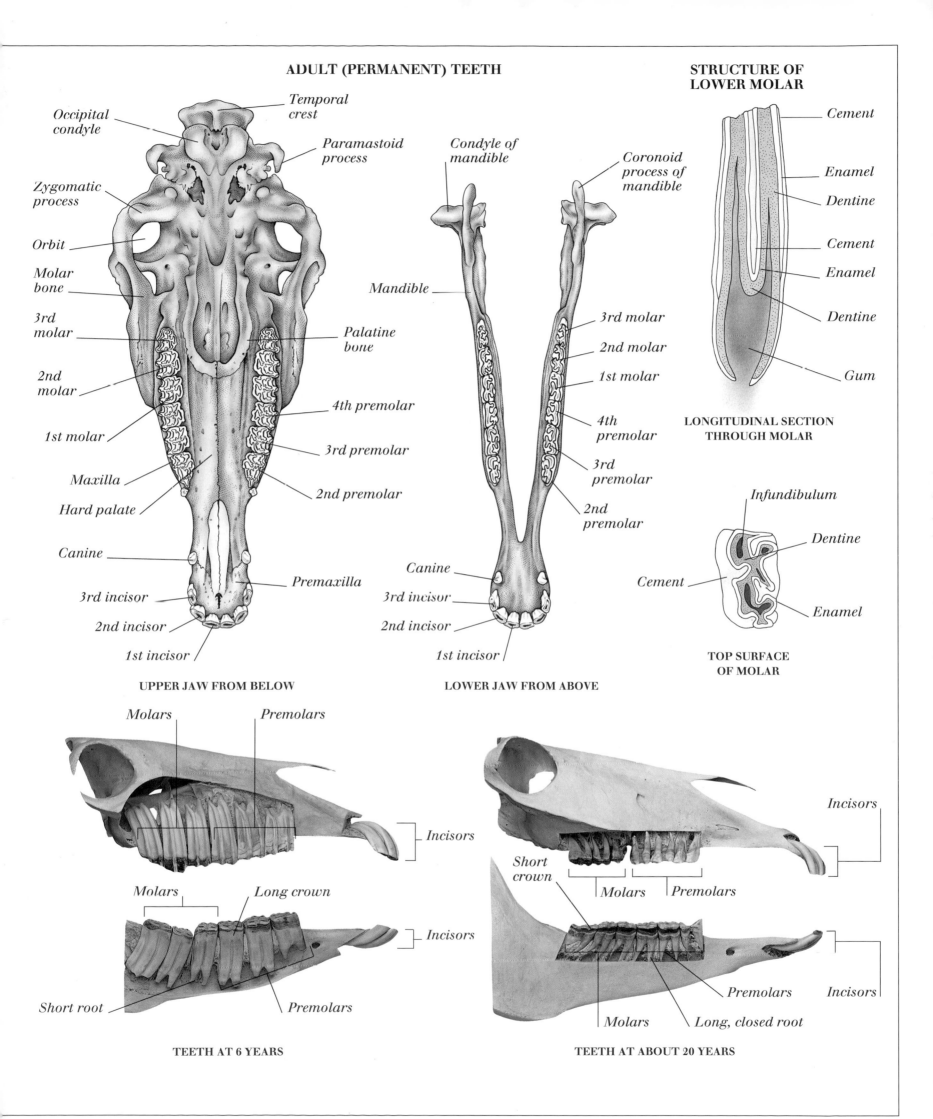

ADULT (PERMANENT) TEETH

Occipital condyle

Temporal crest

Paramastoid process

Zygomatic process

Orbit

Molar bone

3rd molar

2nd molar

1st molar

Maxilla

Hard palate

Canine

3rd incisor

2nd incisor

1st incisor

Palatine bone

4th premolar

3rd premolar

2nd premolar

Premaxilla

UPPER JAW FROM BELOW

Condyle of mandible

Coronoid process of mandible

Mandible

3rd molar

2nd molar

1st molar

4th premolar

3rd premolar

2nd premolar

Canine

3rd incisor

2nd incisor

1st incisor

LOWER JAW FROM ABOVE

STRUCTURE OF LOWER MOLAR

Cement

Enamel

Dentine

Cement

Enamel

Dentine

Gum

LONGITUDINAL SECTION THROUGH MOLAR

Infundibulum

Dentine

Cement

Enamel

TOP SURFACE OF MOLAR

Molars

Premolars

Incisors

Molars

Long crown

Incisors

Short root

Premolars

TEETH AT 6 YEARS

Incisors

Short crown

Molars

Premolars

Incisors

Premolars

Incisors

Molars

Long, closed root

TEETH AT ABOUT 20 YEARS

15

Muscles

THE HORSE'S STAMINA, STRENGTH, AND AGILITY are largely due to a well-developed muscle system and a strong skeleton (see pp. 10-11). Muscle consists of fibrous bands of tissue that can contract and relax to produce movement. The horse has muscles in every part of its body, from inside the eye to the wall of the intestine, and from the heart to the legs. There are two main types of muscles: voluntary and involuntary. Voluntary muscles are consciously controlled by the horse and are responsible for movements such as walking, galloping, and chewing. In contrast, involuntary muscles contract and relax without the horse's conscious control. The heart is made up of a special type of muscle, known as cardiac muscle. Involuntary muscles are responsible for automatic actions, such as changing the size of the pupil in the eye and moving food along the intestine. Most voluntary muscles are large, superficial muscles that lie immediately beneath the skin; these are the muscles shown in the illustrations here. Most involuntary muscles form an integral part of certain organs, such as the stomach. The superficial muscles are attached to the skeleton by cords of dense tissue called tendons, and the bones are connected together by bands of tough fibrous tissue called ligaments.

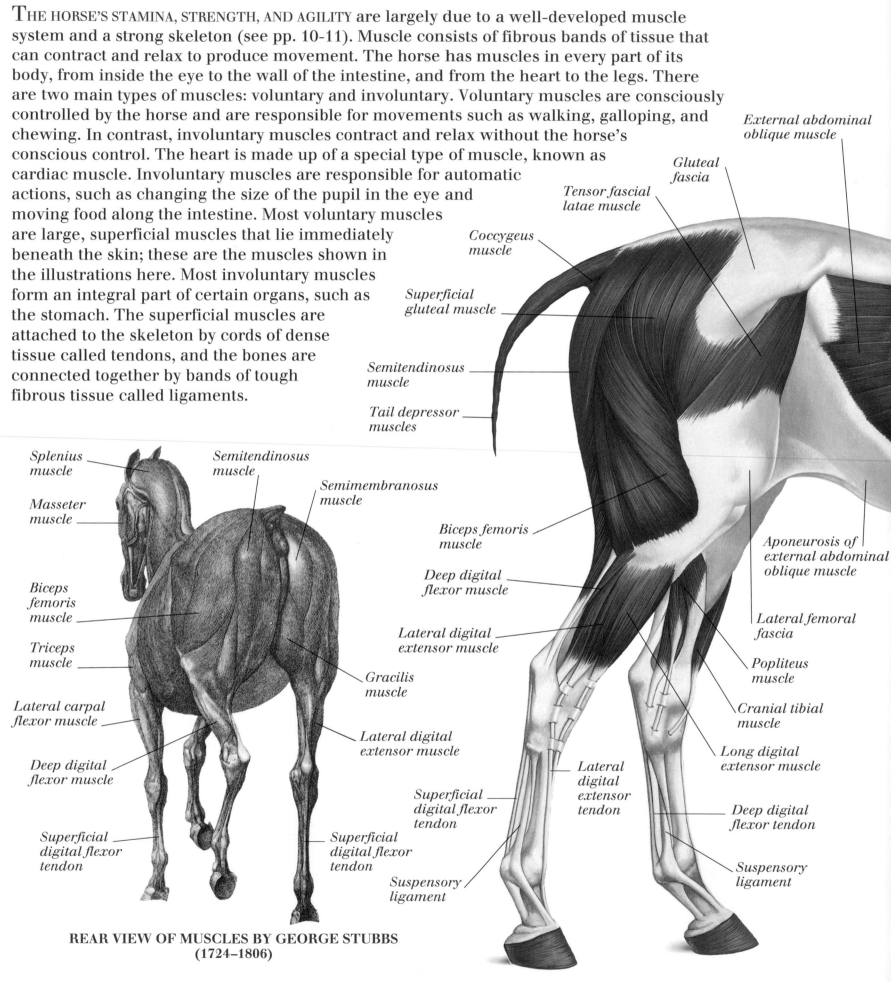

External abdominal oblique muscle

Gluteal fascia

Tensor fascial latae muscle

Coccygeus muscle

Superficial gluteal muscle

Semitendinosus muscle

Tail depressor muscles

Biceps femoris muscle

Deep digital flexor muscle

Lateral digital extensor muscle

Aponeurosis of external abdominal oblique muscle

Lateral femoral fascia

Popliteus muscle

Cranial tibial muscle

Long digital extensor muscle

Lateral digital extensor tendon

Superficial digital flexor tendon

Lateral digital extensor muscle

Deep digital flexor tendon

Suspensory ligament

Splenius muscle

Semitendinosus muscle

Masseter muscle

Semimembranosus muscle

Biceps femoris muscle

Triceps muscle

Gracilis muscle

Lateral carpal flexor muscle

Lateral digital extensor muscle

Deep digital flexor muscle

Superficial digital flexor tendon

Superficial digital flexor tendon

Suspensory ligament

**REAR VIEW OF MUSCLES BY GEORGE STUBBS
(1724–1806)**

16

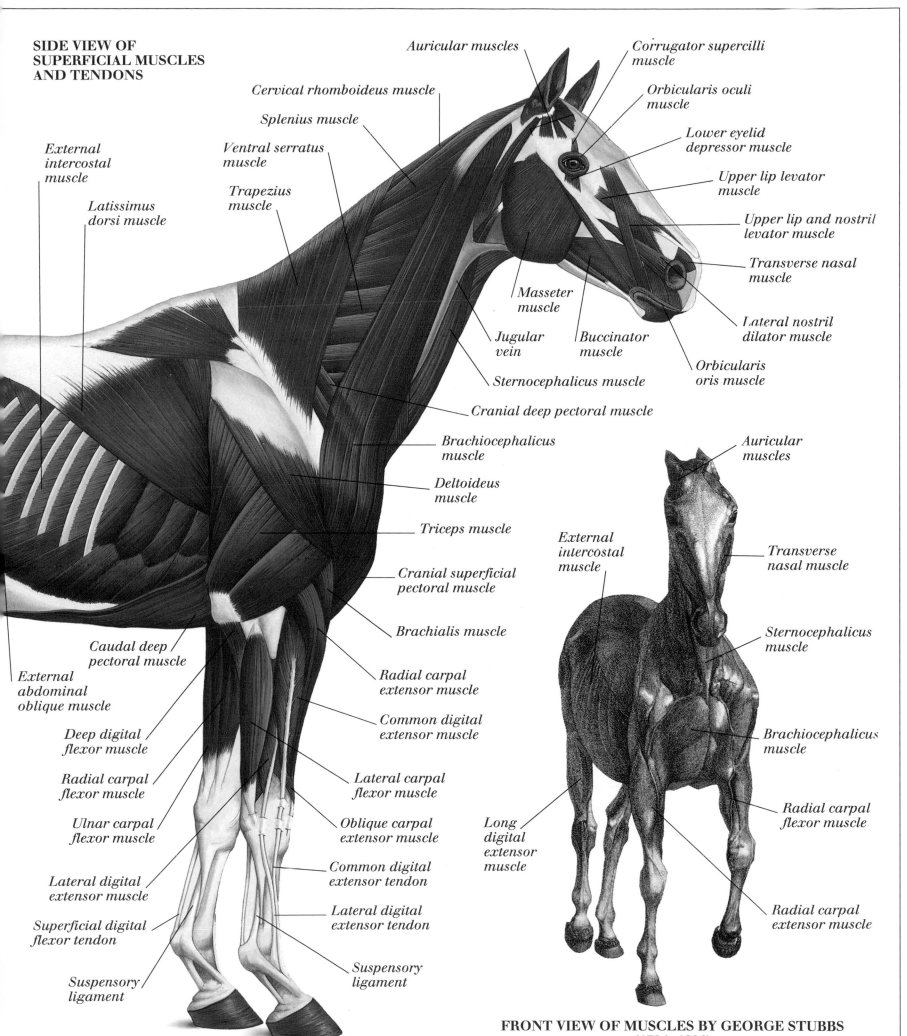

SIDE VIEW OF SUPERFICIAL MUSCLES AND TENDONS

Auricular muscles

Corrugator supercilli muscle

Cervical rhomboideus muscle

Orbicularis oculi muscle

Splenius muscle

Lower eyelid depressor muscle

External intercostal muscle

Ventral serratus muscle

Upper lip levator muscle

Trapezius muscle

Upper lip and nostril levator muscle

Latissimus dorsi muscle

Transverse nasal muscle

Masseter muscle

Lateral nostril dilator muscle

Jugular vein

Buccinator muscle

Orbicularis oris muscle

Sternocephalicus muscle

Cranial deep pectoral muscle

Brachiocephalicus muscle

Auricular muscles

Deltoideus muscle

Triceps muscle

External intercostal muscle

Transverse nasal muscle

Cranial superficial pectoral muscle

Brachialis muscle

Sternocephalicus muscle

Caudal deep pectoral muscle

Radial carpal extensor muscle

Brachiocephalicus muscle

External abdominal oblique muscle

Common digital extensor muscle

Deep digital flexor muscle

Radial carpal flexor muscle

Radial carpal flexor muscle

Lateral carpal flexor muscle

Ulnar carpal flexor muscle

Long digital extensor muscle

Radial carpal extensor muscle

Oblique carpal extensor muscle

Lateral digital extensor muscle

Common digital extensor tendon

Superficial digital flexor tendon

Lateral digital extensor tendon

Suspensory ligament

Suspensory ligament

FRONT VIEW OF MUSCLES BY GEORGE STUBBS (1724–1806)

17

Nervous system

THE NERVOUS SYSTEM is a complex
information processing and storage
network that enables the horse to detect
and react to changes inside and outside
its body; to automatically control various
internal processes, such as the beating of the
heart; and to initiate conscious actions, such
as walking. It consists of two parts: the central
nervous system, composed of the brain and
spinal cord; and the peripheral nervous system,
which includes the sensory organs, such as the eyes
and ears, and the network of nerves that connects the
brain and spinal cord to the rest of the body. The brain
has three main regions: the brainstem, cerebellum, and
cerebrum. The brainstem performs many functions, including
relaying information from the spinal cord and regulating
respiration and blood circulation. The cerebellum controls
balance and the coordination of voluntary muscles. The
cerebrum processes information from the sensory organs,
and is also responsible for many conscious and intelligent
activities. The main function of the spinal cord is to carry
messages to and from the brain, and to mediate certain
reflex actions. The peripheral nervous system carries
messages from sensory organs to the central nervous
system, and transmits messages from the central nervous
system to muscles, organs, and glands throughout the body.

SECTION THROUGH EYE

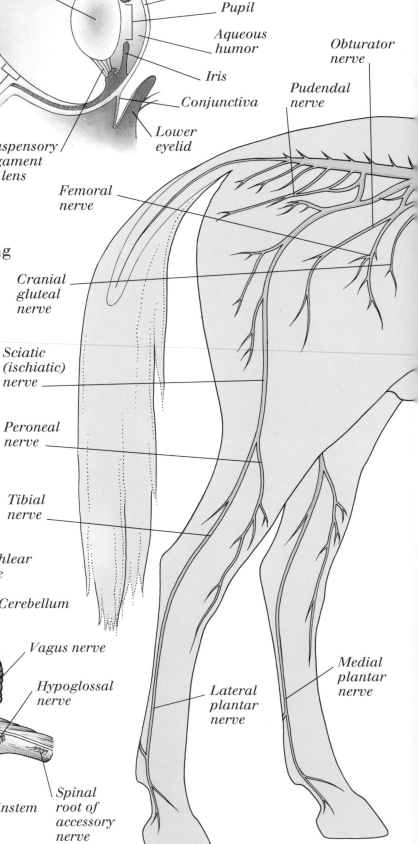

Retina
Lens
Sclera
Vitreous humor
Choroid
Optic nerve
Optic disk
Suspensory ligament of lens
Fornix
Upper eyelid
Eyelash
Corpora nigra
Cornea
Pupil
Aqueous humor
Iris
Conjunctiva
Lower eyelid
Obturator nerve
Pudendal nerve
Femoral nerve
Cranial gluteal nerve
Sciatic (ischiatic) nerve
Peroneal nerve
Tibial nerve
Lateral plantar nerve
Medial plantar nerve

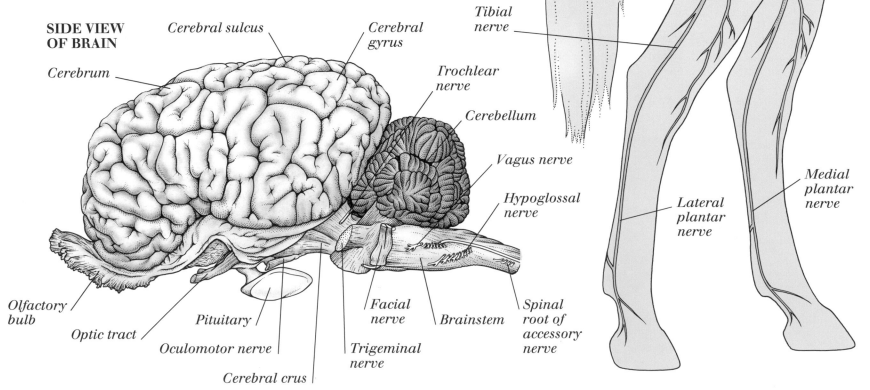

SIDE VIEW OF BRAIN

Cerebral sulcus
Cerebral gyrus
Cerebrum
Trochlear nerve
Cerebellum
Vagus nerve
Hypoglossal nerve
Olfactory bulb
Optic tract
Pituitary
Oculomotor nerve
Cerebral crus
Trigeminal nerve
Facial nerve
Brainstem
Spinal root of accessory nerve

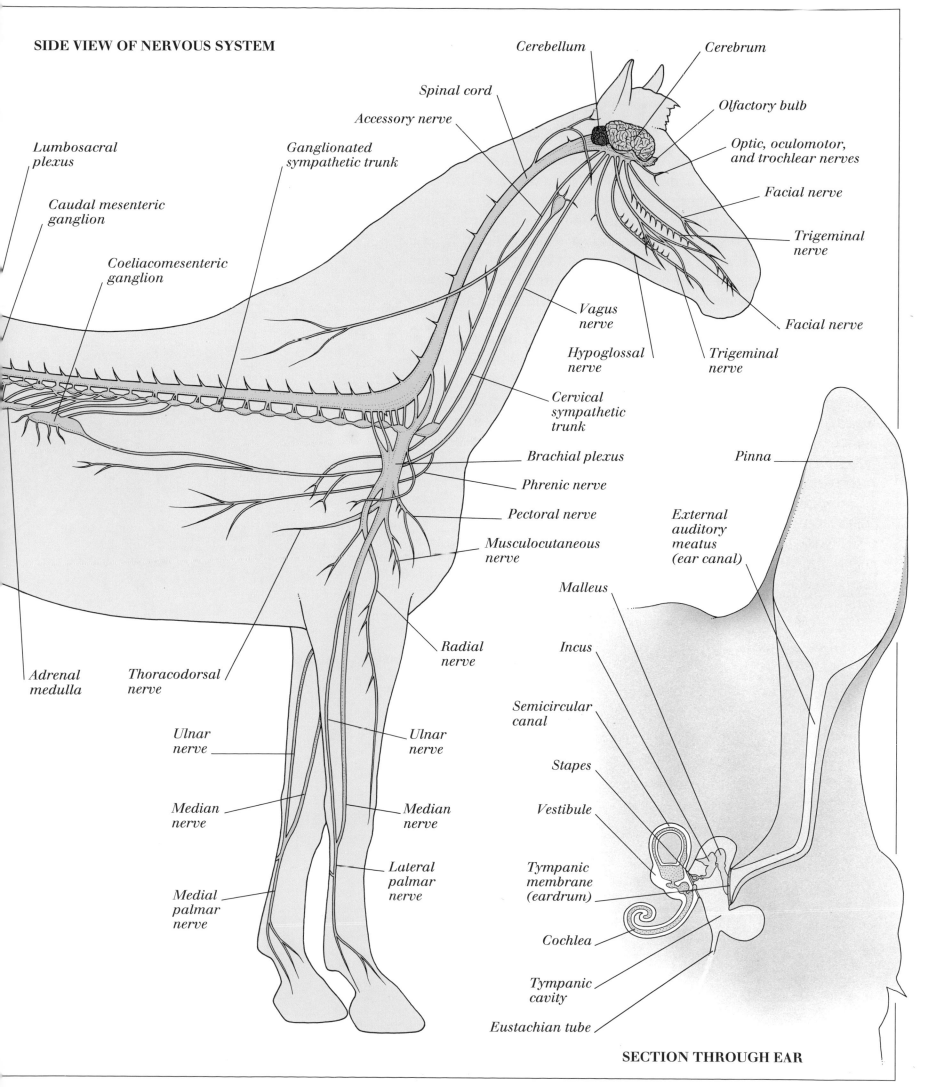

SIDE VIEW OF NERVOUS SYSTEM

Cerebellum

Cerebrum

Spinal cord

Accessory nerve

Olfactory bulb

Lumbosacral plexus

Ganglionated sympathetic trunk

Optic, oculomotor, and trochlear nerves

Facial nerve

Caudal mesenteric ganglion

Trigeminal nerve

Coeliacomesenteric ganglion

Vagus nerve

Facial nerve

Hypoglossal nerve

Trigeminal nerve

Cervical sympathetic trunk

Brachial plexus

Pinna

Phrenic nerve

Pectoral nerve

External auditory meatus (ear canal)

Musculocutaneous nerve

Malleus

Incus

Radial nerve

Semicircular canal

Adrenal medulla

Thoracodorsal nerve

Stapes

Vestibule

Ulnar nerve

Ulnar nerve

Median nerve

Median nerve

Tympanic membrane (eardrum)

Lateral palmar nerve

Medial palmar nerve

Cochlea

Tympanic cavity

Eustachian tube

SECTION THROUGH EAR

19

Respiratory and circulatory systems

THE RESPIRATORY AND CIRCULATORY systems together supply oxygen to, and remove carbon dioxide from, every cell in the horse's body. The circulatory system also carries nutrients and other substances around the body in the blood. The respiratory system consists of the air passages (nasal passages and trachea) and lungs. Air is inhaled into the lungs, and oxygen in the air passes across the thin lung walls and into the blood. Meanwhile, carbon dioxide passes out of the blood into the lungs and is breathed out of the body during exhalation. The circulatory system consists of the heart and blood vessels (arteries, veins, and capillaries). The heart pumps deoxygenated blood (shown in blue in the illustrations) to the lungs, where it becomes oxygenated (shown in red) and returns to the heart. The oxygenated blood is then pumped through arteries to the rest of the body. The blood passes from the arteries into the capillaries where the body cells take up the oxygen and release carbon dioxide and other waste products into the blood. The blood (now deoxygenated) returns through the veins to the heart, and the cycle continues.

SECTION THROUGH LUNGS

Trachea
Tracheobronchial lymph nodes
Left bronchus
Right bronchus
Right lobe
Left lobe
Outline of accessory lobe (dotted line)

SECTION THROUGH HEART

Cranial vena cava
Aorta
Pectinate muscles
Pulmonary trunk
Right atrium
Aortic valve
Right coronary artery
Pulmonary vein
Right atrioventricular valve
Left atrium
Chordae tendineae
Great cardiac vein
Septomarginal trabecula
Left coronary artery
Right ventricle
Left atrioventricular valve
Ventricular septum
Chordae tendineae
Left ventricle
Papillary muscle
Septomarginal trabecula

Caudal gluteal artery
Internal iliac artery
Internal iliac vein
Cranial gluteal artery
Caudal mesenteric artery
External iliac artery
External iliac vein
Femoral vein
Femoral artery
Saphenous vein
Cranial tibial vein
Caudal mesenteric vein
Popliteal artery
Saphenous artery
Cranial tibial artery
Medial plantar artery
Lateral plantar metatarsal artery
Lateral plantar metatarsal vein
Medial dorsal metatarsal vein
Medial plantar digital vein
Lateral digital artery
Medial plantar digital artery
Lateral digital vein
Coronary venous plexus

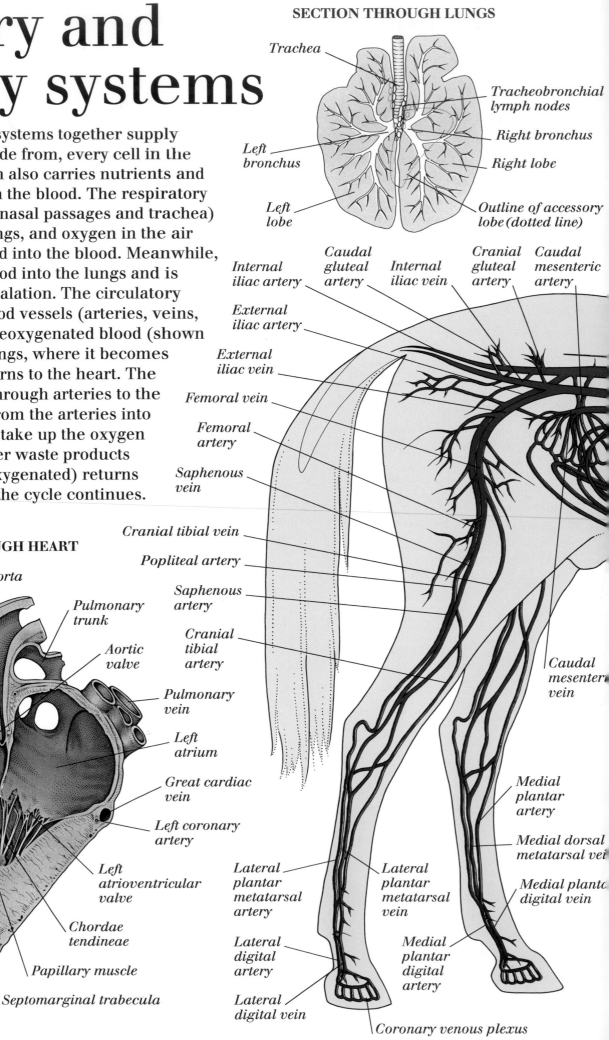

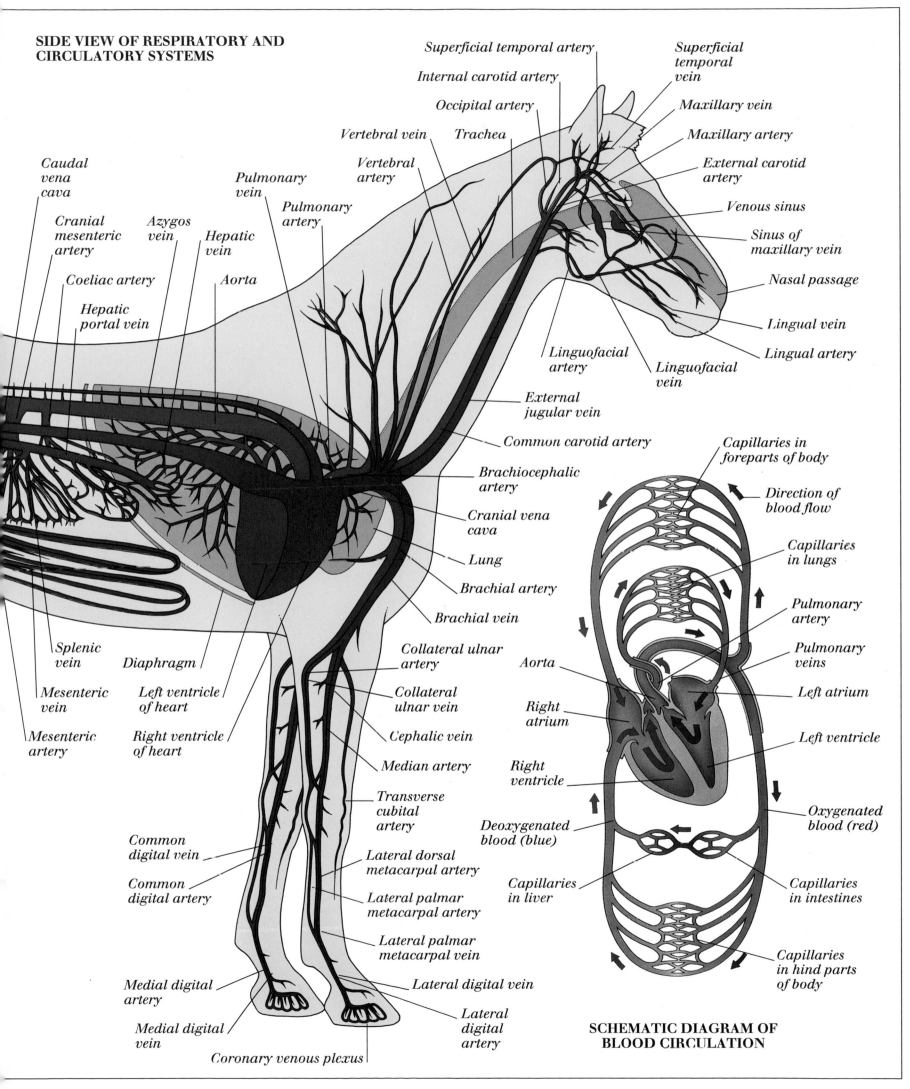

SIDE VIEW OF RESPIRATORY AND CIRCULATORY SYSTEMS

Superficial temporal artery

Internal carotid artery

Occipital artery

Vertebral vein

Trachea

Vertebral artery

Pulmonary vein

Pulmonary artery

Caudal vena cava

Cranial mesenteric artery

Azygos vein

Hepatic vein

Coeliac artery

Aorta

Hepatic portal vein

Superficial temporal vein

Maxillary vein

Maxillary artery

External carotid artery

Venous sinus

Sinus of maxillary vein

Nasal passage

Lingual vein

Lingual artery

Linguofacial artery

Linguofacial vein

External jugular vein

Common carotid artery

Brachiocephalic artery

Cranial vena cava

Lung

Brachial artery

Brachial vein

Collateral ulnar artery

Collateral ulnar vein

Cephalic vein

Median artery

Transverse cubital artery

Splenic vein

Mesenteric vein

Mesenteric artery

Diaphragm

Left ventricle of heart

Right ventricle of heart

Common digital vein

Common digital artery

Medial digital artery

Medial digital vein

Lateral dorsal metacarpal artery

Lateral palmar metacarpal artery

Lateral palmar metacarpal vein

Lateral digital vein

Lateral digital artery

Coronary venous plexus

Capillaries in foreparts of body

Direction of blood flow

Capillaries in lungs

Pulmonary artery

Pulmonary veins

Left atrium

Aorta

Right atrium

Left ventricle

Right ventricle

Deoxygenated blood (blue)

Capillaries in liver

Oxygenated blood (red)

Capillaries in intestines

Capillaries in hind parts of body

SCHEMATIC DIAGRAM OF BLOOD CIRCULATION

21

Digestive system

THE DIGESTIVE SYSTEM breaks down food by chemical and physical processes so that it can be absorbed by the body tissues and used to provide raw materials for energy, growth, and cell maintenance. The system consists of the alimentary tract (which extends from the mouth to the anus) and associated organs and glands that secrete digestive juices. Digestion begins in the mouth, where grass (the staple food of horses) is physically ground down by chewing and chemically broken down with saliva. Physical breakdown continues as food is churned and pushed along the alimentary tract by muscular contractions of the tract wall. Chemical breakdown also continues as food is digested by gastric juices in the stomach and by enzymes in the small intestine. Further breakdown occurs in the cecum and colon, where microorganisms produce enzymes that break down cellulose (a major constituent of grass). The products of digestion are absorbed into the blood mainly from the small intestine and cecum, although fluids are absorbed chiefly from the colon. Indigestible food is stored in the rectum until it is expelled through the anus as feces.

Esophagus

Liver

Molars

Incisors

Premolars

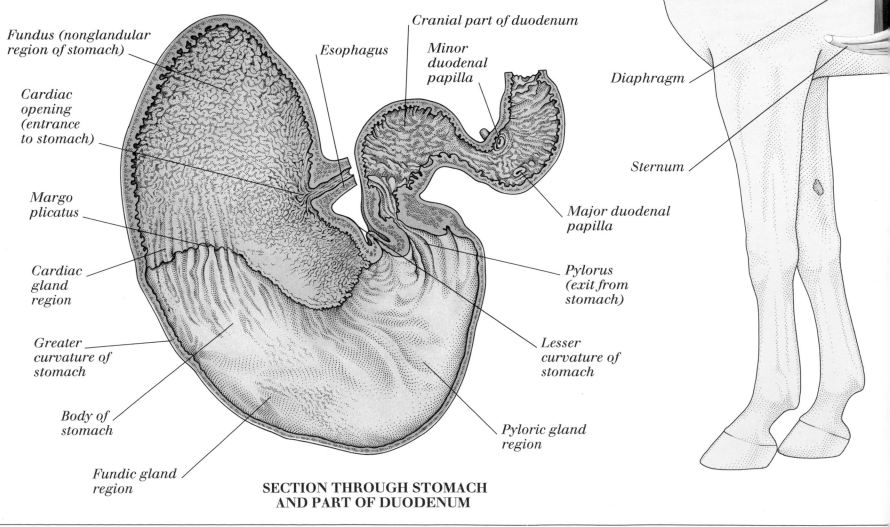

Fundus (nonglandular region of stomach)

Esophagus

Cranial part of duodenum

Minor duodenal papilla

Cardiac opening (entrance to stomach)

Margo plicatus

Cardiac gland region

Greater curvature of stomach

Body of stomach

Fundic gland region

Major duodenal papilla

Pylorus (exit from stomach)

Lesser curvature of stomach

Pyloric gland region

Diaphragm

Sternum

SECTION THROUGH STOMACH AND PART OF DUODENUM

SIDE VIEW OF DIGESTIVE SYSTEM

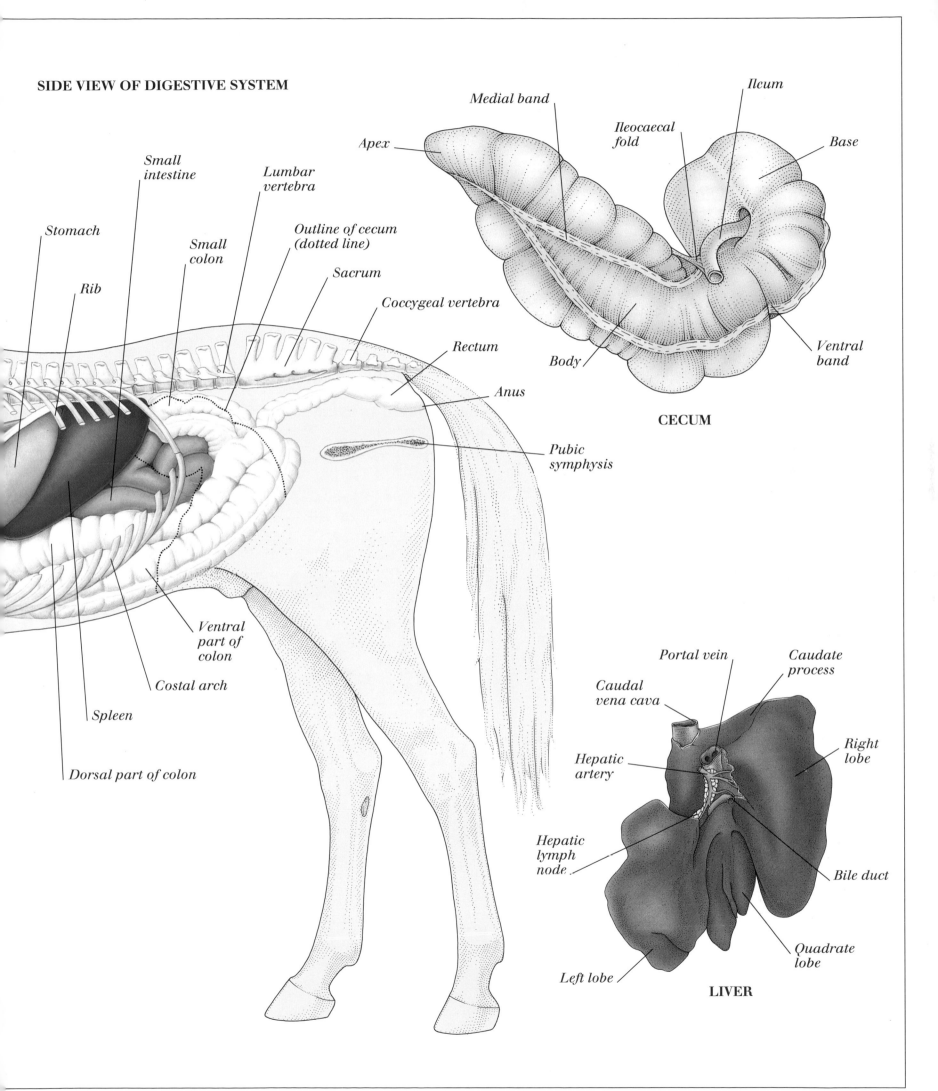

Medial band

Ileum

Apex

Ileocaecal fold

Base

Small intestine

Lumbar vertebra

Stomach

Small colon

Outline of cecum (dotted line)

Sacrum

Rib

Coccygeal vertebra

Rectum

Body

Ventral band

Anus

CECUM

Pubic symphysis

Ventral part of colon

Costal arch

Spleen

Dorsal part of colon

Portal vein

Caudate process

Caudal vena cava

Right lobe

Hepatic artery

Hepatic lymph node

Bile duct

Left lobe

Quadrate lobe

LIVER

23

Urinogenital system

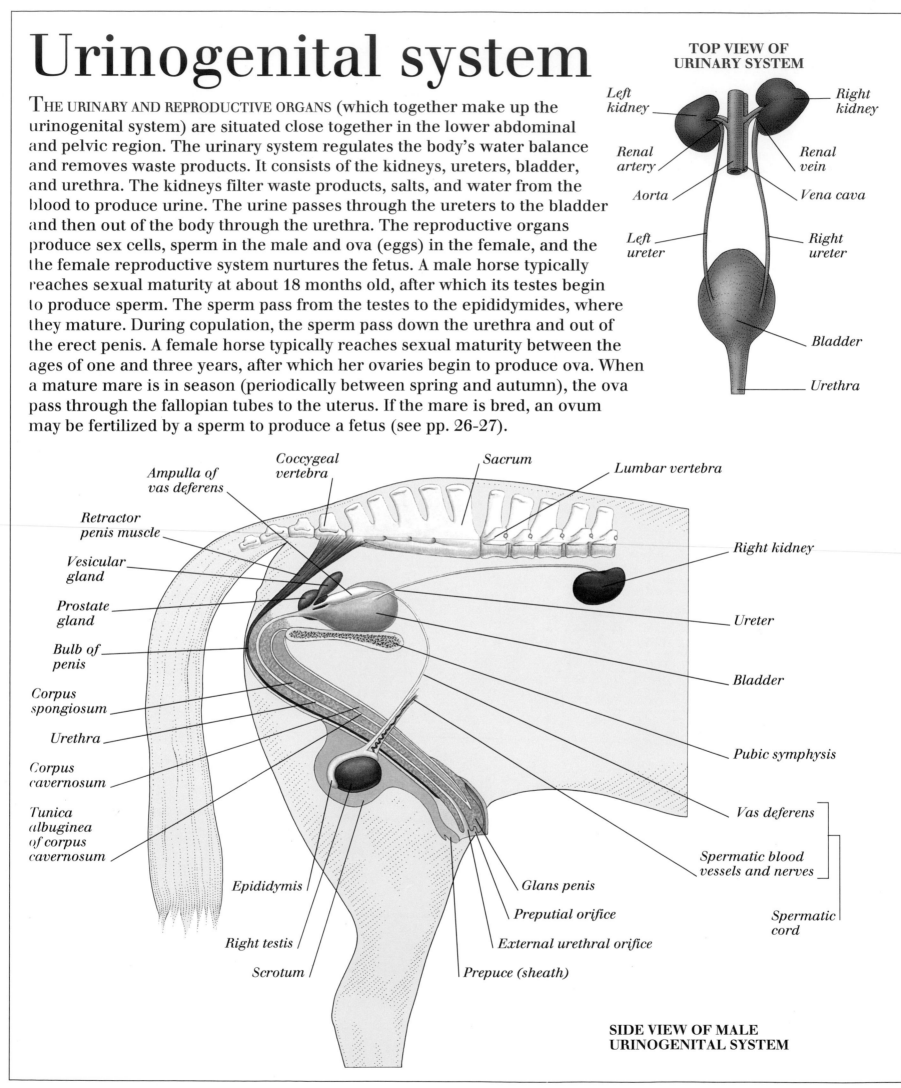

THE URINARY AND REPRODUCTIVE ORGANS (which together make up the urinogenital system) are situated close together in the lower abdominal and pelvic region. The urinary system regulates the body's water balance and removes waste products. It consists of the kidneys, ureters, bladder, and urethra. The kidneys filter waste products, salts, and water from the blood to produce urine. The urine passes through the ureters to the bladder and then out of the body through the urethra. The reproductive organs produce sex cells, sperm in the male and ova (eggs) in the female, and the the female reproductive system nurtures the fetus. A male horse typically reaches sexual maturity at about 18 months old, after which its testes begin to produce sperm. The sperm pass from the testes to the epididymides, where they mature. During copulation, the sperm pass down the urethra and out of the erect penis. A female horse typically reaches sexual maturity between the ages of one and three years, after which her ovaries begin to produce ova. When a mature mare is in season (periodically between spring and autumn), the ova pass through the fallopian tubes to the uterus. If the mare is bred, an ovum may be fertilized by a sperm to produce a fetus (see pp. 26-27).

TOP VIEW OF URINARY SYSTEM

Left kidney

Right kidney

Renal artery

Renal vein

Aorta

Vena cava

Left ureter

Right ureter

Bladder

Urethra

Ampulla of vas deferens

Coccygeal vertebra

Sacrum

Lumbar vertebra

Retractor penis muscle

Right kidney

Vesicular gland

Prostate gland

Ureter

Bulb of penis

Bladder

Corpus spongiosum

Urethra

Pubic symphysis

Corpus cavernosum

Tunica albuginea of corpus cavernosum

Vas deferens

Spermatic blood vessels and nerves

Epididymis

Glans penis

Preputial orifice

Spermatic cord

Right testis

External urethral orifice

Scrotum

Prepuce (sheath)

SIDE VIEW OF MALE URINOGENITAL SYSTEM

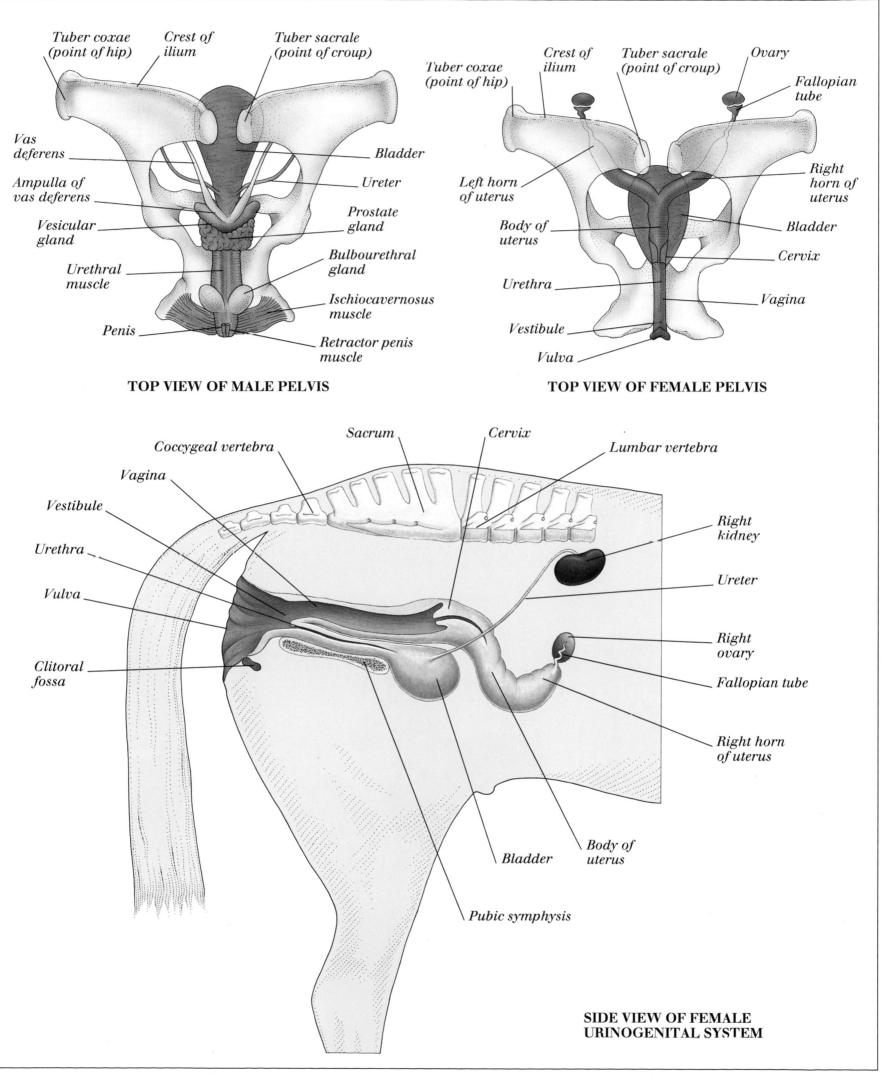

TOP VIEW OF MALE PELVIS

Tuber coxae (point of hip)
Crest of ilium
Tuber sacrale (point of croup)
Vas deferens
Ampulla of vas deferens
Vesicular gland
Urethral muscle
Penis
Bladder
Ureter
Prostate gland
Bulbourethral gland
Ischiocavernosus muscle
Retractor penis muscle

TOP VIEW OF FEMALE PELVIS

Crest of ilium
Tuber sacrale (point of croup)
Ovary
Tuber coxae (point of hip)
Fallopian tube
Left horn of uterus
Right horn of uterus
Body of uterus
Bladder
Cervix
Urethra
Vagina
Vestibule
Vulva

SIDE VIEW OF FEMALE URINOGENITAL SYSTEM

Coccygeal vertebra
Sacrum
Cervix
Lumbar vertebra
Vagina
Vestibule
Urethra
Right kidney
Vulva
Ureter
Clitoral fossa
Right ovary
Fallopian tube
Right horn of uterus
Bladder
Body of uterus
Pubic symphysis

Development and growth

Mares that are sexually mature come into season (also known as estrus) every year between spring and autumn. When in season, it is possible for a mare to mate and to conceive a foal (it is rare for a mare to have twins). The fetus takes about 11 months to develop in the mare's uterus; this is known as the gestation period. At the end of the gestation period, the foal is ready to be born. The mare usually lies down to give birth. When the foal is being born, its front feet normally emerge first, followed by its head and then the rest of its body. Immediately after the birth, the mare gets up and licks her newborn foal clean, which also helps the foal's circulation and breathing. Within about an hour of being born, the foal is able to stand up, and it begins to suck milk from its mother's teats. The foal lives on its mother's milk alone for the first two months and then gradually begins to eat grass until it is fully weaned at about six months old. Foals and young horses—known as fillies if they are female, or colts if they are male—grow relatively quickly. They reach adult size between the age of four and five years, by which time they also have their full set of adult teeth (see pp. 14-15).

TEN-YEAR-OLD SHIRE MARE AND HER FIVE-WEEK-OLD FOAL

DEVELOPMENT OF FETUS IN THE UTERUS

Developing umbilical cord

Chorion

Allantoic cavity filled with fluid

Amniotic cavity filled with fluid

Fetus

Amnion

2 MONTHS

Hairs appear around lips

Umbilical cord fully developed

Soft, rubbery hooves form

4 MONTHS

DEVELOPMENT OF A FOAL

Large cranium

Eyes open from birth

Short face

Short, small body

Small mouth

Wide-based stance for stability

Long, thin legs

Small, soft hooves

NEWBORN FOAL

Upright, feathery mane

Large eyes

Short, bushy tail

Large nostrils

FOAL AT 2 WEEKS

Soft, woolly coat, known as milk hair

Croup higher than withers

Cannon bone becomes longer

Upright stance

FOAL AT 5 WEEKS

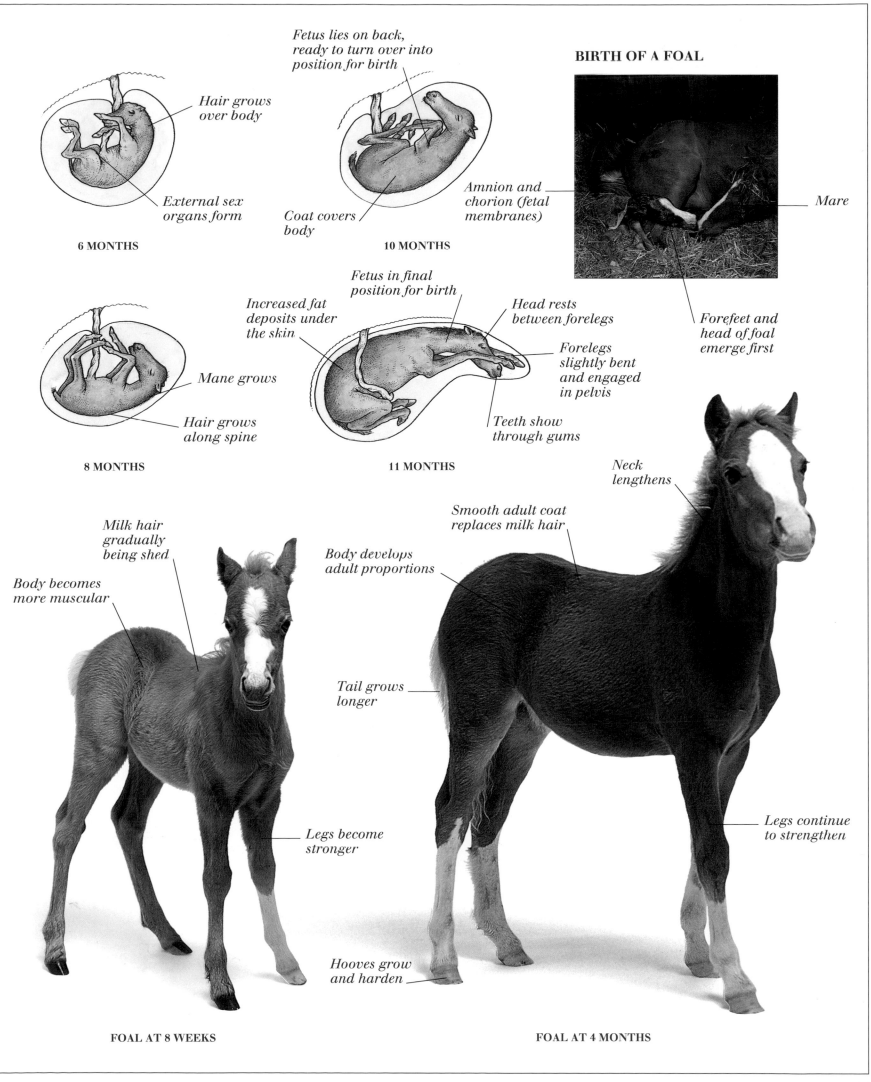

Hair grows
over body

External sex
organs form

6 MONTHS

Fetus lies on back,
ready to turn over into
position for birth

Coat covers
body

Amnion and
chorion (fetal
membranes)

10 MONTHS

BIRTH OF A FOAL

Mare

Forefeet and
head of foal
emerge first

Increased fat
deposits under
the skin

Mane grows

Hair grows
along spine

8 MONTHS

Fetus in final
position for birth

Head rests
between forelegs

Forelegs
slightly bent
and engaged
in pelvis

Teeth show
through gums

11 MONTHS

Neck
lengthens

Smooth adult coat
replaces milk hair

Milk hair
gradually
being shed

Body develops
adult proportions

Body becomes
more muscular

Tail grows
longer

Legs continue
to strengthen

Legs become
stronger

Hooves grow
and harden

FOAL AT 8 WEEKS

FOAL AT 4 MONTHS

Ponies 1

A PONY CAN BE DEFINED AS ANY HORSE that is 14.2 hands (58 in) or less in height, but there is more to a pony than its stature. Typical characteristics of ponies are deep, compact bodies; great strength in relation to their height; long, thick manes and tails; good endurance; and a natural hardiness that enables them to thrive in harsh environments. Some breeds—the Falabella, for example—have horselike characteristics and are therefore sometimes considered to be horses rather than ponies despite their small size. There are many breeds of ponies, and their features vary depending on the conditions in the region where they evolved. Ponies whose natural habitats are the inhospitable terrain and cold climates of northern Europe and Asia—the Dartmoor pony, for example—tend to be small and stocky with thick coats. In contrast, ponies such as the Caspian (see pp. 30-31) that originate in the warmer climates of the Middle East and Africa tend to have longer, lighter bodies and thinner coats. Most ponies are easy to train, and are put to a wide variety of uses. For example, the New Forest and Australian ponies are suitable for riding. Other ponies, such as the Norwegian Fjord, can also be used as pack animals, or for agricultural and light harness work.

FALABELLA

Small ears

Well-defined withers

Long head

Strong, slender legs

Long, sloping shoulders

AMERICAN SHETLAND PONY
Origin: US

Short, compact body

Short, thick neck

Small head

Long, thick tail

Sloping shoulders

Short, sturdy legs

BARDIGIANO
Origin: Italy

Thick mane

Long neck

Low withers

Broad forehead

Straight profile

Wide sloping croup

Long, straight back

Wide nostrils

Sloping croup

Long, sloping shoulders

Long, thick tail

Broad, deep chest

Deep, compact body

Strong, slender legs

Short, sturdy legs

Powerful, compact body

NEW FOREST PONY
Origin: England

NORWEGIAN FJORD
Origin: Norway

ROCKY MOUNTAIN PONY
Origin: US

- Long, flaxen tail
- Low withers
- Long neck
- Long, flaxen mane
- Strong, slender legs

WELSH PONY
Origin: Wales

- Powerful hindquarters
- Long neck
- Small ears
- Sloping shoulders
- Strong, slender legs

HIGHLAND PONY
Origin: Scotland

- Sloping croup
- Dorsal stripe
- Long neck
- Small ears
- Deep, compact body
- Short cannon bone
- Feathering on legs

BASHKIR
Origin: Russian Federation

- Short, flat back
- Low withers
- Long mane
- Short, thick neck
- Sloping shoulders
- Short cannon bone
- Short, sturdy legs

DALES PONY
Origin: England

- Powerful hindquarters
- Short back
- Low withers
- Long neck
- Small ears
- Sloping shoulders
- Strong, slender legs
- Feathering on legs

SHETLAND PONY
Origin: Scotland

- Short, strong back
- Short neck
- Small ears
- Deep, compact body
- Small head
- Long, sloping shoulders
- Short, strong legs

- Dorsal stripe
- Black and silver mane
- Small ears
- Straight profile
- Wide nostrils
- Low withers
- Thick jowl
- Dun coat
- Broad, deep chest
- Zebra-barred legs

DARTMOOR PONY
Origin: England

- Short, strong neck
- Small ears
- Small head
- Sloping croup
- Short back
- Low withers
- Long, thick mane
- Long, sloping shoulders
- Broad, deep chest
- Long, thick tail
- Deep, compact body
- Strong, slender legs
- Short cannon bone
- Feathering on legs

Ponies 2

Icelandic Horse

Small ears

Short back

Deep, compact body

Thick mane

Short, strong legs

Short cannon bone

Long, thick tail

ICELANDIC HORSE
Origin: Iceland

Exmoor Pony

Toad (hooded) eye

Small ears

Thick mane

Long back

Sloping croup

Wide nostrils

Broad, deep chest

Thick tail

Short cannon bone

Deep, compact body

Short, sturdy legs

EXMOOR PONY
Origin: England

Welsh Mountain Pony (large horse)

Broad forehead

Long, arched neck

Straight profile

Well-defined withers

Tapered muzzle

Wide nostrils

Broad, deep chest

Sloping shoulders

Strong, slender legs

Short cannon bone

Fell Pony

Small ears

Long, thick mane

Deep, compact body

Sloping shoulders

Short, sturdy legs

Long, thick tail

FELL PONY
Origin: England

Welsh Mountain Pony

Small ears

Deep, compact body

Sloping croup

Long, sloping shoulders

Long, thick tail

WELSH MOUNTAIN PONY
Origin: Wales

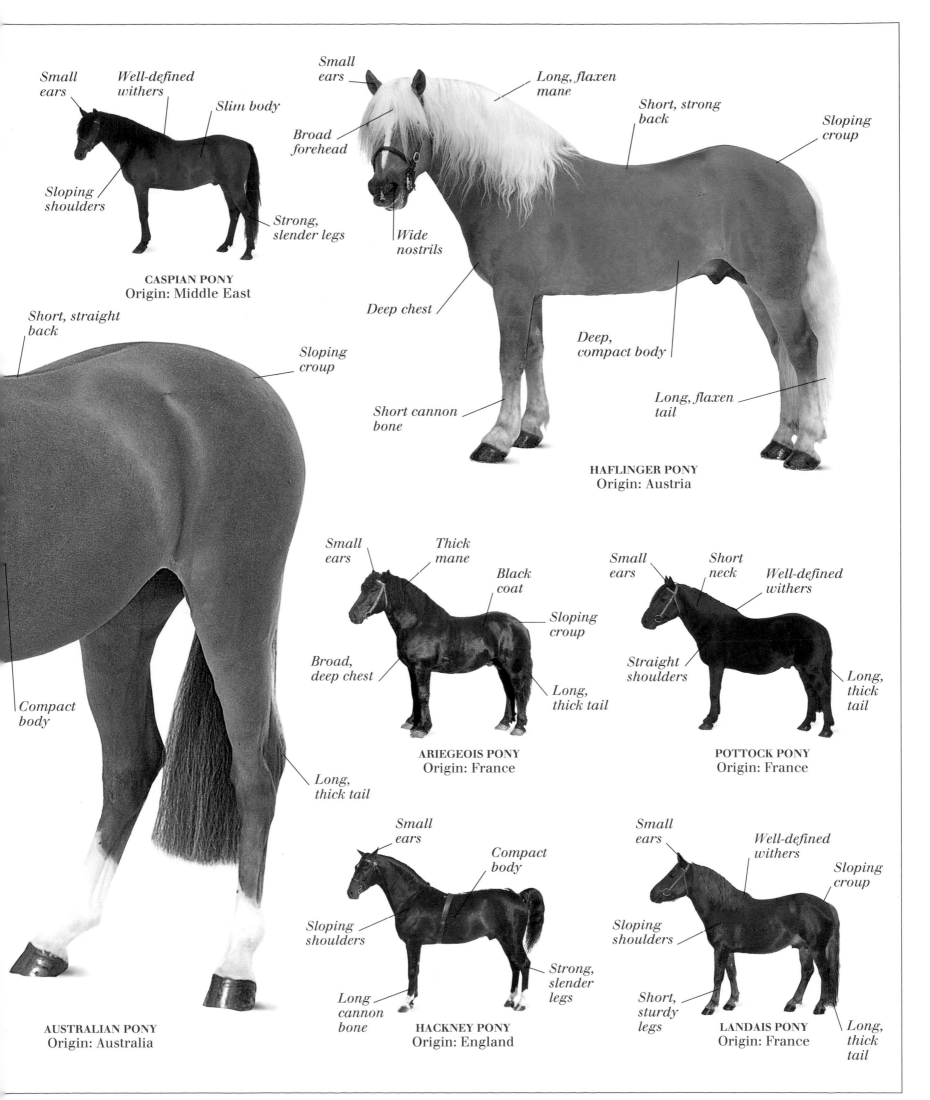

Small ears

Well-defined withers

Slim body

Sloping shoulders

Strong, slender legs

CASPIAN PONY
Origin: Middle East

Small ears

Broad forehead

Wide nostrils

Deep chest

Long, flaxen mane

Short, strong back

Sloping croup

Deep, compact body

Long, flaxen tail

Short cannon bone

HAFLINGER PONY
Origin: Austria

Short, straight back

Sloping croup

Compact body

Long, thick tail

AUSTRALIAN PONY
Origin: Australia

Small ears

Thick mane

Black coat

Sloping croup

Broad, deep chest

Long, thick tail

ARIEGEOIS PONY
Origin: France

Small ears

Short neck

Well-defined withers

Straight shoulders

Long, thick tail

POTTOCK PONY
Origin: France

Small ears

Compact body

Sloping shoulders

Strong, slender legs

Long cannon bone

HACKNEY PONY
Origin: England

Small ears

Well-defined withers

Sloping croup

Sloping shoulders

Short, sturdy legs

Long, thick tail

LANDAIS PONY
Origin: France

Light horses 1

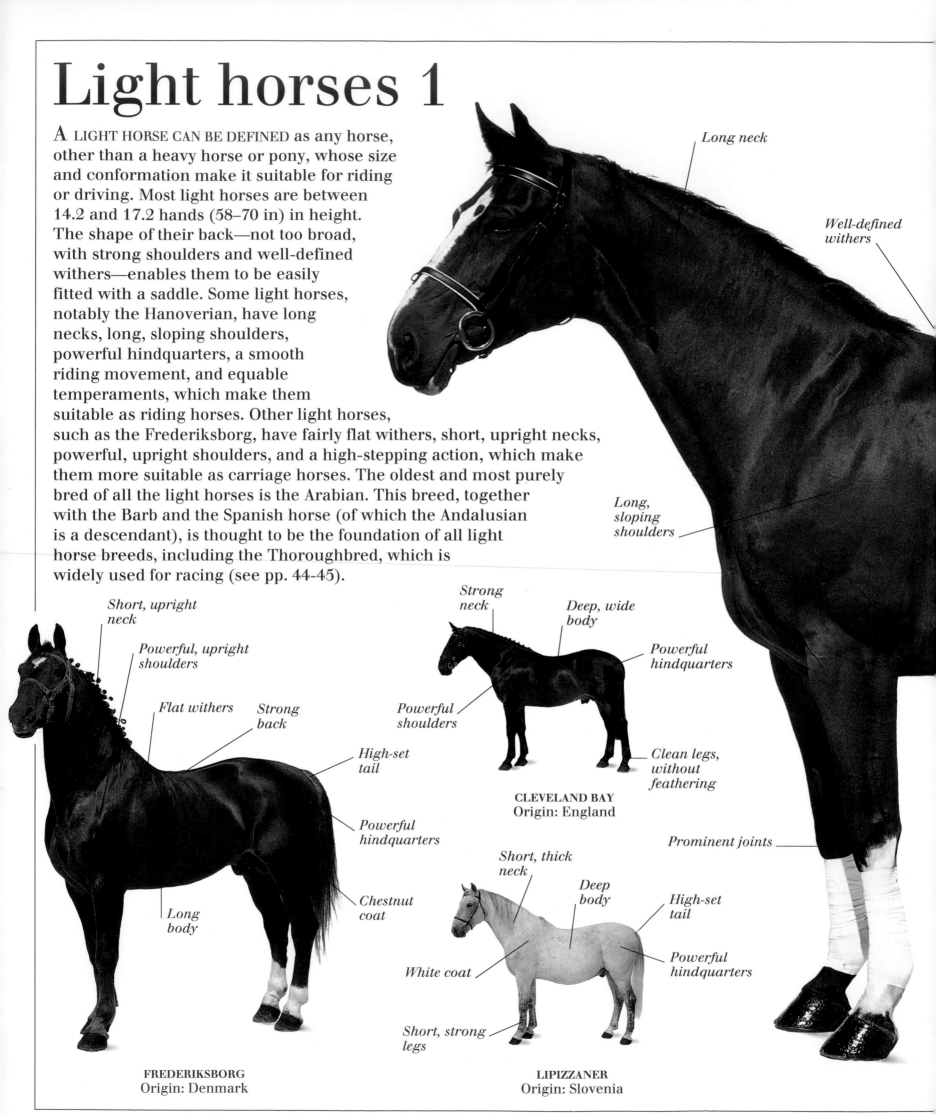

A LIGHT HORSE CAN BE DEFINED as any horse, other than a heavy horse or pony, whose size and conformation make it suitable for riding or driving. Most light horses are between 14.2 and 17.2 hands (58–70 in) in height. The shape of their back—not too broad, with strong shoulders and well-defined withers—enables them to be easily fitted with a saddle. Some light horses, notably the Hanoverian, have long necks, long, sloping shoulders, powerful hindquarters, a smooth riding movement, and equable temperaments, which make them suitable as riding horses. Other light horses, such as the Frederiksborg, have fairly flat withers, short, upright necks, powerful, upright shoulders, and a high-stepping action, which make them more suitable as carriage horses. The oldest and most purely bred of all the light horses is the Arabian. This breed, together with the Barb and the Spanish horse (of which the Andalusian is a descendant), is thought to be the foundation of all light horse breeds, including the Thoroughbred, which is widely used for racing (see pp. 44-45).

Long neck

Well-defined withers

Long, sloping shoulders

Prominent joints

Short, upright neck

Powerful, upright shoulders

Flat withers

Strong back

High-set tail

Powerful hindquarters

Chestnut coat

Long body

FREDERIKSBORG
Origin: Denmark

Strong neck

Deep, wide body

Powerful hindquarters

Powerful shoulders

Clean legs, without feathering

CLEVELAND BAY
Origin: England

Short, thick neck

Deep body

High-set tail

White coat

Powerful hindquarters

Short, strong legs

LIPIZZANER
Origin: Slovenia

Well-defined withers

Deep, compact body

Powerful hindquarters

Sloping shoulders

TENNESSEE WALKING HORSE
Origin: US

Well-defined withers

Compact body

Powerful hindquarters

Sloping shoulders

MORGAN
Origin: US

Long, arched neck

Well-defined withers

Powerful hindquarters

Sloping shoulders

SADDLEBRED
Origin: US

Strong back

Powerful hindquarters

Deep, compact body

Short cannon bone

HANOVERIAN
Origin: Germany

Short, wide head

Long neck

Well-defined withers

Powerful hindquarters

Small muzzle

Sloping shoulders

QUARTER HORSE
Origin: US

Well-defined withers

High croup

Powerful hindquarters

Sloping shoulders

STANDARDBRED
Origin: US

Light horses 2

Fine, silky tail

Powerful hindquarters

Short back

Well-defined withers

Dish face

Sloping shoulders

Compact body

Flat knees

Short cannon bone

ARABIAN
Origin: Middle East

Powerful hindquarters

Long, narrow body

Long neck

Sloping shoulders

AKHAL-TEKE
Origin: Turkmenistan

Straight back

Strong neck

Powerful hindquarters

Sickle-shaped hindleg

Upright shoulders

KABARDIN
Origin: Northern Caucasus

Powerful hindquarters

Compact body

Sloping shoulders

SHAGYA ARABIAN
Origin: Hungary

Powerful hindquarters

Compact body

Well-defined withers

Sloping shoulders

ANGLO-ARAB
Origins: UK and France

High croup

Short, strong back

Strong neck

Deep, compact body

Upright shoulders

BARB
Origin: Morocco

Powerful hindquarters

Wide, straight back

Short, upright shoulders

DON
Origin: Russian Federation

Powerful hindquarters

Well-defined withers

Sloping shoulders

Short cannon bone

TRAKEHNER
Origin: Poland

Powerful hindquarters

Short, straight back

Well-defined withers

Short, sloping shoulders

BUDONNY
Origin: Russian Federation

Powerful hindquarters

Compact body

Sloping shoulders

TERSK
Origin: Northern Caucasus

Powerful hindquarters

Strong back

Well-defined withers

Sloping shoulders

NONIUS
Origin: Hungary

Powerful hindquarters

Short, strong back

Sloping shoulders

Short cannon bone

DUTCH WARMBLOOD
Origin: Netherlands

Powerful hindquarters

Compact body

Strong neck

Upright shoulders

FRENCH TROTTER
Origin: France

Powerful hindquarters

Strong, arched neck

Long, wavy mane

Strong, sloping shoulders

Compact body

Powerful hindquarters

Well-defined withers

Long neck

Sloping shoulders

SELLE FRANCAIS
Origin: France

ANDALUSIAN
Origin: Spain

Heavy horses 1

HEAVY HORSES ARE LARGE, POWERFUL EQUINES that have been used in agriculture and for hauling heavy loads. They typically stand between 14.2 and 18 hands high (58–72 in), and some of the larger breeds—the Shire, for example—may weigh as much as 2,200 lb (1,000 kg). Heavy horses are characterized by relatively short backs and legs; broad, powerful chests; good temperaments; and great strength and stamina. They grow a thick winter coat that is shed in summer. Some heavy horses have fine hair (known as feathering) around their lower legs. They are easily managed and used for a variety of work. Heavy horses were traditionally used in warfare, and modern breeds are thought to be descended from horses that were used for carrying heavily armored medieval knights into battle. More recently, heavy horses such as the Percheron (see pp. 38-39) were used in World War I to pull supply wagons and heavy artillery. Heavy horses have also been used for various types of agricultural work, particularly plowing. In industry, they were used for hauling loads such as wagons and barges. The work carried out by heavy horses is now done mostly by machines, although they are sometimes still used in farming and for pulling brewer's drays.

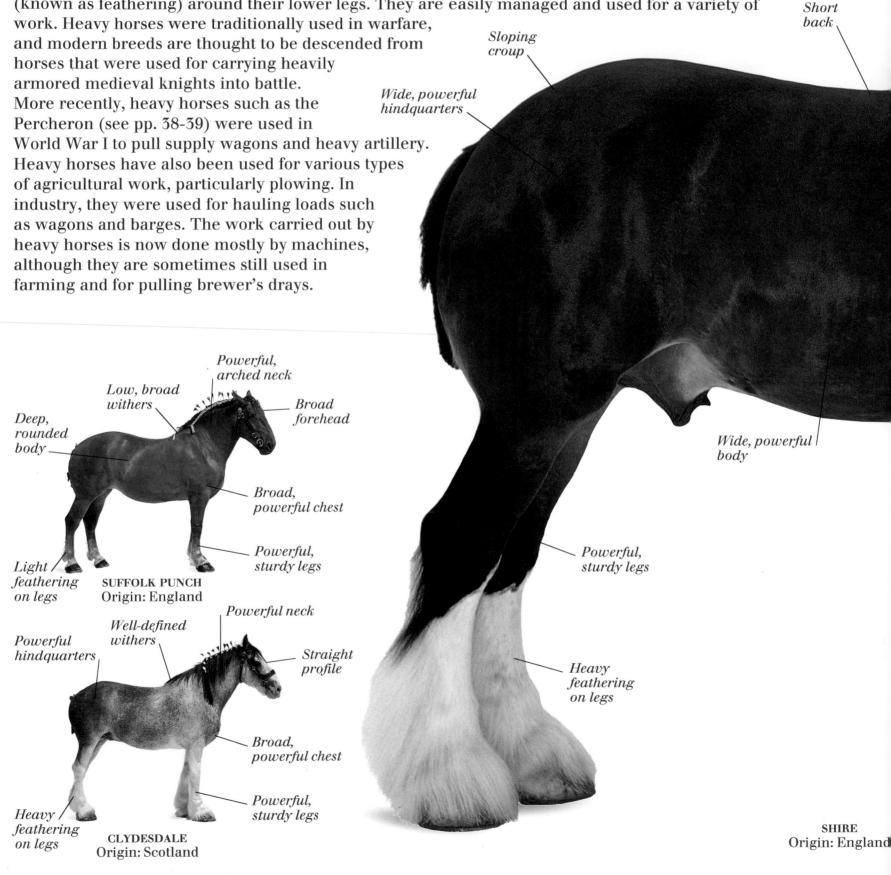

Sloping croup

Wide, powerful hindquarters

Short back

Wide, powerful body

Powerful, sturdy legs

Heavy feathering on legs

SHIRE
Origin: England

Powerful, arched neck

Low, broad withers

Broad forehead

Deep, rounded body

Broad, powerful chest

Powerful, sturdy legs

Light feathering on legs

SUFFOLK PUNCH
Origin: England

Powerful neck

Well-defined withers

Straight profile

Powerful hindquarters

Broad, powerful chest

Powerful, sturdy legs

Heavy feathering on legs

CLYDESDALE
Origin: Scotland

Long, powerful neck

Low, broad withers

Broad forehead

Roman (convex) nose

Wide, deep shoulders

Broad, powerful chest

Forelegs set well apart

Long cannon bone

Powerful, arched neck

Straight profile

Powerful hindquarters

Broad, powerful chest

Light feathering on legs

Powerful, short legs

BRETON
Origin: France

Powerful, arched neck

Straight profile

Low, wide withers

Long, sloping shoulders

Powerful, short legs

Short cannon bone

Light feathering on legs

BOULONNAIS
Origin: France

Short, strong back

Powerful, arched neck

Powerful hindquarters

Broad, powerful chest

Powerful, sturdy legs

Forelegs set well apart

Light feathering on legs

BRABANT
Origin: Belgium

Powerful hindquarters

Short, strong back

Powerful neck

Broad, powerful chest

Powerful, sturdy legs

NORMAN COB
Origin: France

Powerful neck

Short, flat back

Powerful hindquarters

Deep, powerful chest

Powerful, sturdy legs

Forelegs set well apart

Light feathering on legs

ITALIAN HEAVY DRAFT
Origin: Italy

Deep, rounded body

Powerful, thick neck

Powerful hindquarters

Broad, powerful chest

Powerful, sturdy legs

Heavy feathering on legs

JUTLAND
Origin: Denmark

Heavy horses 2

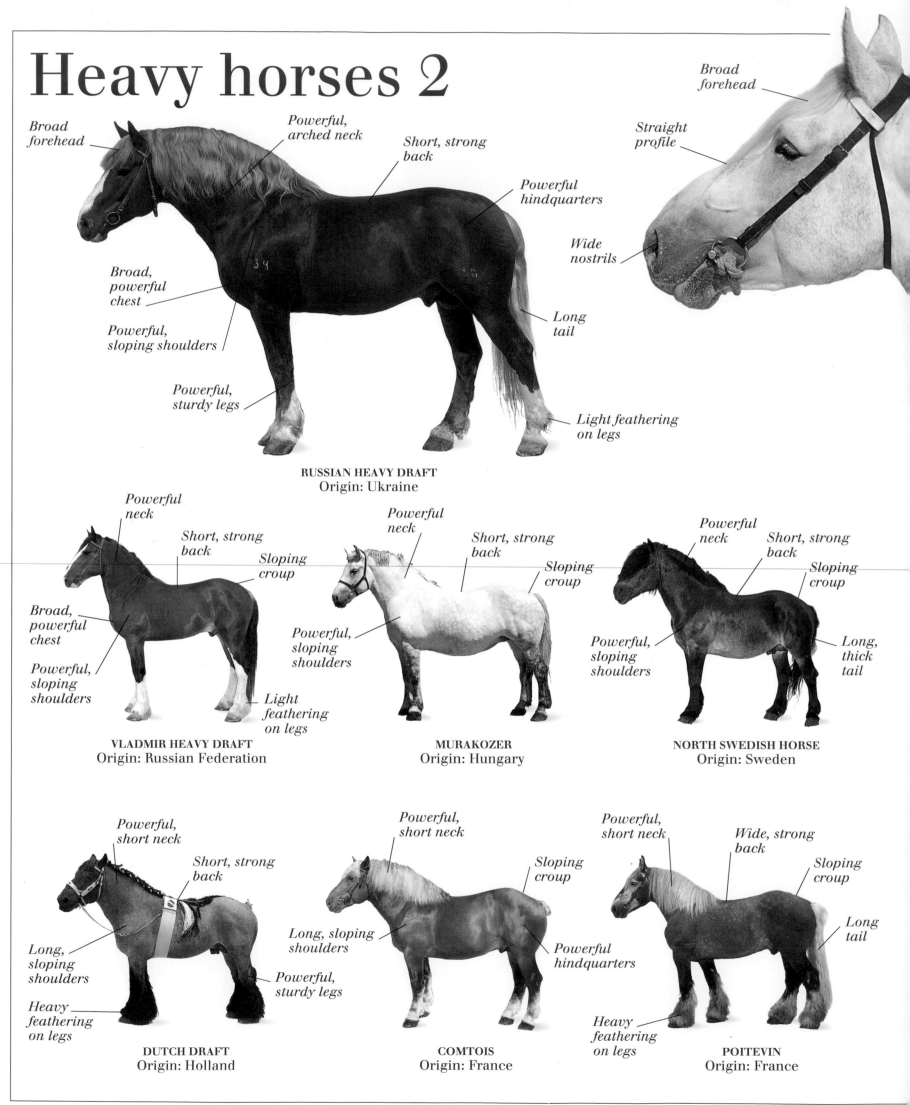

Broad forehead

Powerful, arched neck

Short, strong back

Powerful hindquarters

Broad, powerful chest

Wide nostrils

Straight profile

Broad forehead

Powerful, sloping shoulders

Long tail

Powerful, sturdy legs

Light feathering on legs

RUSSIAN HEAVY DRAFT
Origin: Ukraine

Powerful neck

Short, strong back

Sloping croup

Broad, powerful chest

Powerful, sloping shoulders

Light feathering on legs

VLADMIR HEAVY DRAFT
Origin: Russian Federation

Powerful neck

Short, strong back

Sloping croup

Powerful, sloping shoulders

MURAKOZER
Origin: Hungary

Powerful neck

Short, strong back

Sloping croup

Powerful, sloping shoulders

Long, thick tail

NORTH SWEDISH HORSE
Origin: Sweden

Powerful, short neck

Short, strong back

Long, sloping shoulders

Heavy feathering on legs

Powerful, sturdy legs

DUTCH DRAFT
Origin: Holland

Powerful, short neck

Sloping croup

Long, sloping shoulders

Powerful hindquarters

COMTOIS
Origin: France

Powerful, short neck

Wide, strong back

Sloping croup

Long tail

Heavy feathering on legs

POITEVIN
Origin: France

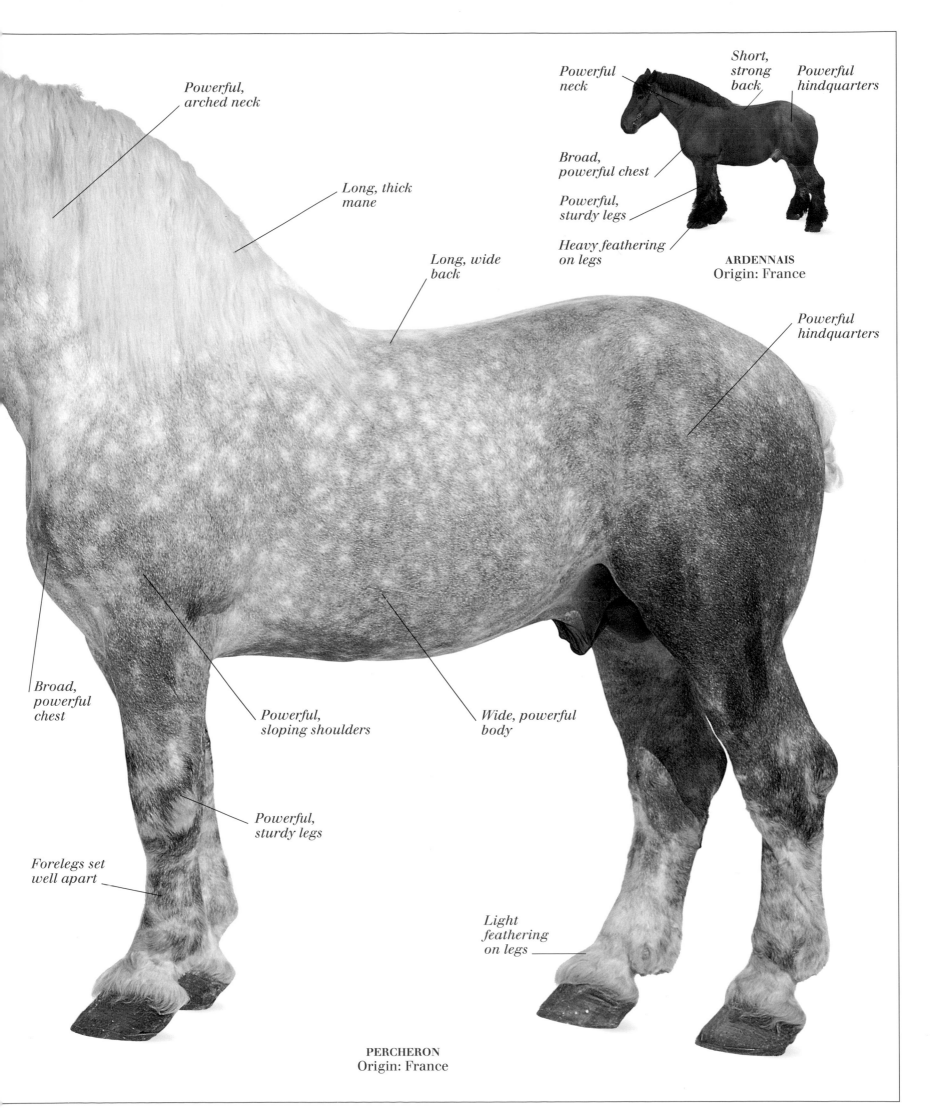

Powerful,
arched neck

Long, thick
mane

Long, wide
back

Powerful
neck

Short,
strong
back

Powerful
hindquarters

Broad,
powerful chest

Powerful,
sturdy legs

Heavy feathering
on legs

ARDENNAIS
Origin: France

Powerful
hindquarters

Broad,
powerful
chest

Powerful,
sloping shoulders

Wide, powerful
body

Powerful,
sturdy legs

Forelegs set
well apart

Light
feathering
on legs

PERCHERON
Origin: France

Gait

THE HORSE HAS FOUR NATURAL GAITS (PACES): walk, trot, canter, and gallop. The walk is a four-beat gait—four footfalls (beats) can be heard in each stride. Each stride is of equal length, and at least two feet are on the ground at the same time. The sequence of footfalls while walking (beginning with the left hindleg) is: left hind, left fore, right hind, and right fore. The trot is a two-beat gait in which the legs move as two diagonal pairs. The first beat occurs as the left fore and right hind touch the ground (the left diagonal). The second beat occurs as the right fore and left hind touch the ground (the right diagonal). The canter is a three-beat gait with a moment of suspension when all four hooves are off the ground. The sequence of footfalls while cantering (beginning with the left hindleg) is: left hind, left fore and right hind (the left diagonal), and right fore. The gallop is the horse's fastest pace and is a four-beat gait. The sequence of footfalls while galloping (beginning with the left hindleg) is: left hind, right hind, left fore, and right fore, followed by a period of suspension with all hooves off the ground. As well as the natural gaits, there are various specialized gaits, such as pacing. Most common in harness racing, pacing has two beats, with the legs moving in lateral pairs: left fore and left hind, followed by right fore and right hind.

PACING IN HARNESS RACING

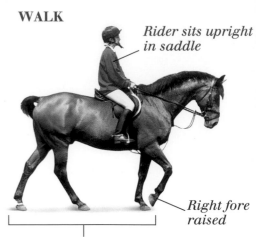

WALK

Rider sits upright in saddle

Right fore raised

Left hind, right hind, and left fore on ground

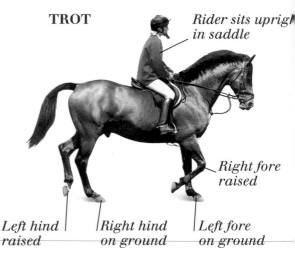

TROT

Rider sits upright in saddle

Right fore raised

Left hind raised

Right hind on ground

Left fore on ground

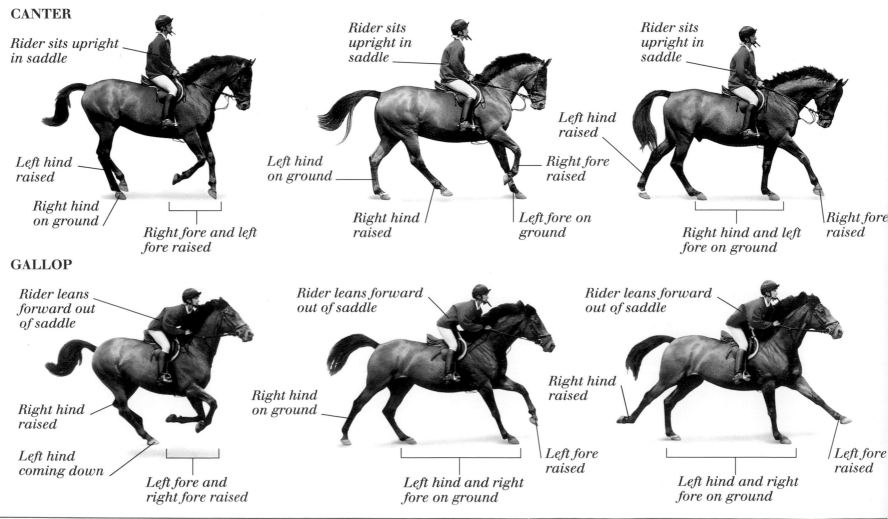

CANTER

Rider sits upright in saddle

Left hind raised

Right hind on ground

Right fore and left fore raised

Rider sits upright in saddle

Left hind on ground

Right hind raised

Left fore on ground

Rider sits upright in saddle

Left hind raised

Right fore raised

Right hind and left fore on ground

Right fore raised

GALLOP

Rider leans forward out of saddle

Right hind raised

Left hind coming down

Left fore and right fore raised

Rider leans forward out of saddle

Right hind on ground

Left hind and right fore on ground

Left fore raised

Rider leans forward out of saddle

Right hind raised

Left hind and right fore on ground

Left fore raised

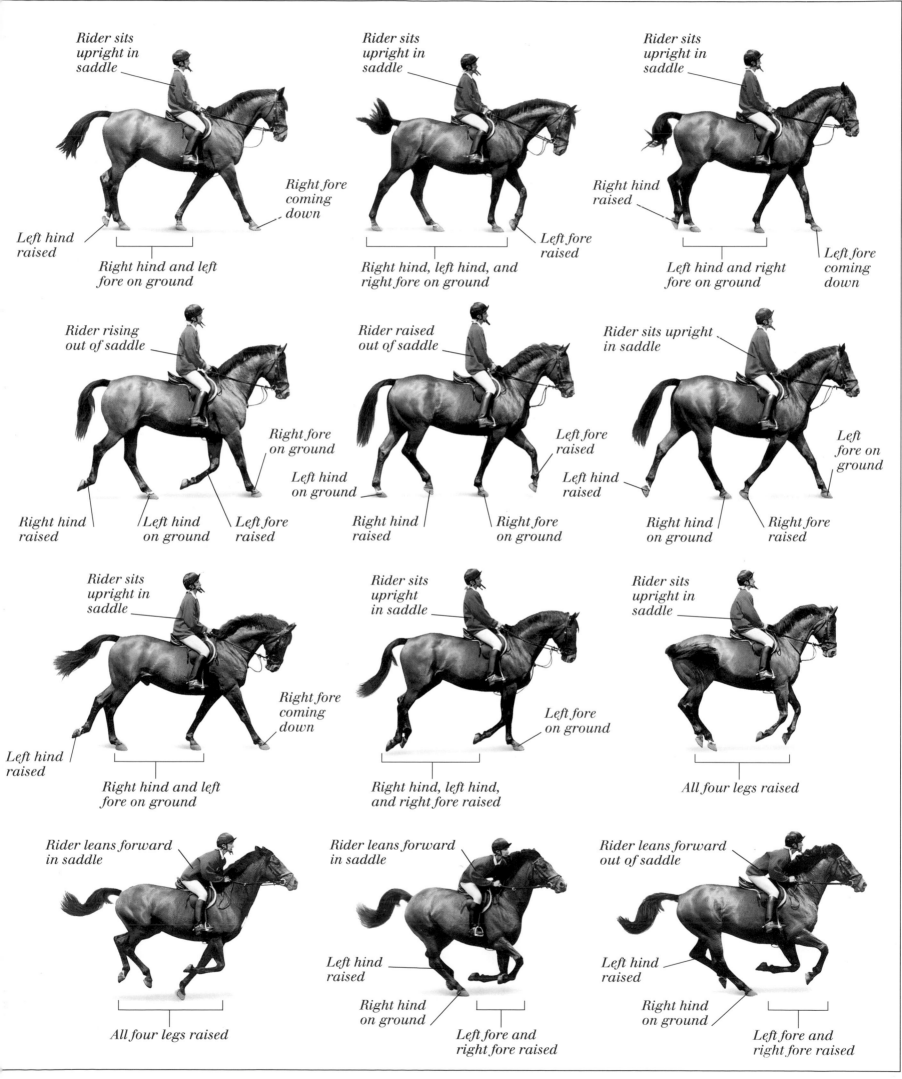

Rider sits upright in saddle

Left hind raised

Right fore coming down

Right hind and left fore on ground

Rider sits upright in saddle

Left fore raised

Right hind, left hind, and right fore on ground

Rider sits upright in saddle

Right hind raised

Left fore coming down

Left hind and right fore on ground

Rider rising out of saddle

Right fore on ground

Right hind raised

Left hind on ground

Left fore raised

Rider raised out of saddle

Left fore raised

Left hind on ground

Right hind raised

Right fore on ground

Rider sits upright in saddle

Left fore on ground

Left hind raised

Right hind on ground

Right fore raised

Rider sits upright in saddle

Left hind raised

Right fore coming down

Right hind and left fore on ground

Rider sits upright in saddle

Left fore on ground

Right hind, left hind, and right fore raised

Rider sits upright in saddle

All four legs raised

Rider leans forward in saddle

All four legs raised

Rider leans forward in saddle

Left hind raised

Right hind on ground

Left fore and right fore raised

Rider leans forward out of saddle

Left hind raised

Right hind on ground

Left fore and right fore raised

41

Jumping

JUMPING IS AN IMPORTANT PART of many equestrian sports, such as show jumping and eventing, which includes cross country jumping. In cross country jumping, the course is usually designed to take advantage of the natural terrain, including features such as water and ditches. Water jumps are among

HORSE AND RIDER JUMPING FENCE

the most difficult obstacles because they often involve several stages; for example, the horse may have to jump over a fence in the water and then jump out of the water onto a sloping bank. There are two main types of show jumping fence: uprights, such as basic upright planks, poles, and walls; and spreads, such as triple bars, hog's backs, and oxers. Uprights are typically between 3 ft (0.9 m) and 6 ft (1.8 m) high, and spreads between 2 ft 6 in (0.8 m) and

6 ft 6 in (2 m) wide. Most show jumping fences consist of wooden stands, known as standards, that support poles or planks. Some parts of the fence—poles, for example—are designed to fall down on impact, to prevent injury to the horse and rider. On the approach to any fence, the horse balances itself and then thrusts forward and upward with its hindlegs. As the horse clears the fence, its legs are folded under its body, with its head and neck stretched to their full extent. The rider leans forward and allows the horse to move its head and neck freely, to avoid impeding its natural jumping action. The horse lands first on one foreleg, then regains its balance as its other legs reach the ground.

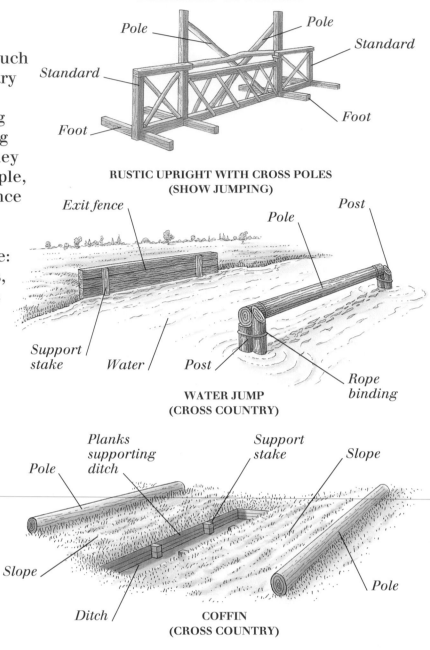

EXAMPLES OF FENCES

Pole

Pole

Standard

Standard

Foot

Foot

RUSTIC UPRIGHT WITH CROSS POLES (SHOW JUMPING)

Exit fence

Pole

Post

Support stake

Water

Post

Rope binding

WATER JUMP (CROSS COUNTRY)

Planks supporting ditch

Support stake

Slope

Pole

Slope

Ditch

Pole

COFFIN (CROSS COUNTRY)

HORSE JUMPING AN OXER

Rider starts to straighten

Horse folds legs under body

Rider leans forward

Rider straightens

Horse extends forelegs

Horse jumps

Rider leans forward

Rider leans forward

Rider starts to lean forward

Horse lands

Horse starts to jump

Rider sits upright

Horse starts to stride away

Horse prepares to jump

Back fence

Oxer

Front fence

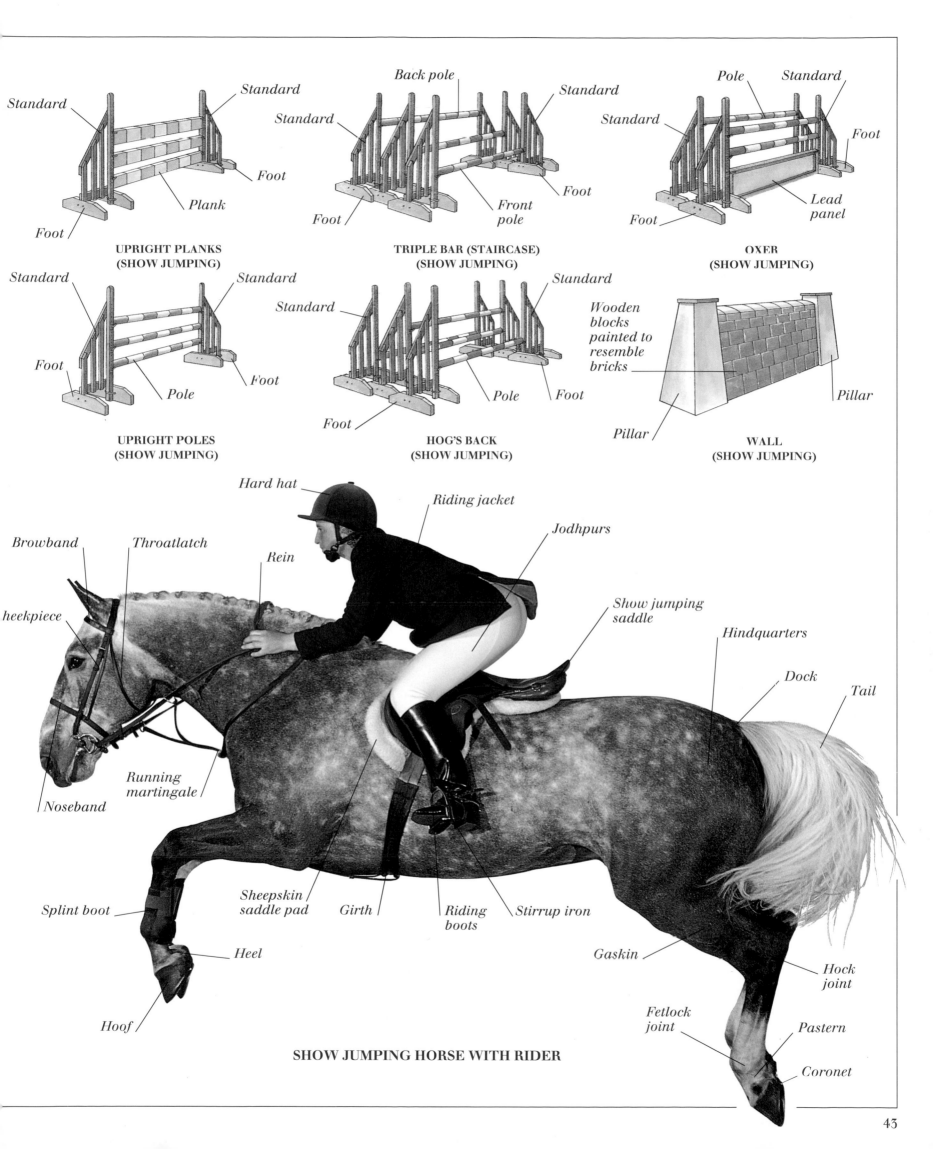

Standard   **Standard**

Foot   **Foot**   **Plank**

**UPRIGHT PLANKS
(SHOW JUMPING)**

Back pole   **Standard**

Standard

Foot   **Front pole**   **Foot**

**TRIPLE BAR (STAIRCASE)
(SHOW JUMPING)**

Pole   **Standard**

Standard   **Foot**

Foot   **Lead panel**

**OXER
(SHOW JUMPING)**

Standard   **Standard**

Foot   **Pole**   **Foot**

**UPRIGHT POLES
(SHOW JUMPING)**

Standard   **Standard**

Foot   **Pole**   **Foot**

**HOG'S BACK
(SHOW JUMPING)**

Wooden blocks painted to resemble bricks

Pillar   **Pillar**

**WALL
(SHOW JUMPING)**

Hard hat   **Riding jacket**

Jodhpurs

Browband   **Throatlatch**

Rein

Show jumping saddle

Hindquarters

heekpiece

Dock   **Tail**

Noseband

Running martingale

Splint boot

Sheepskin saddle pad   **Girth**   **Riding boots**   **Stirrup iron**

Gaskin

Hock joint

Heel

Hoof

Fetlock joint

Pastern

Coronet

SHOW JUMPING HORSE WITH RIDER

Racing

FROM ANCIENT GREEK TIMES TO THE PRESENT DAY, horse racing has been one of the most popular equine sports. Modern horse racing takes several different forms. The simplest is flat racing, in which jockeys ride horses that race against each other on a track without jumps. Races with jumps are divided into two types: steeplechases and hurdle races. In steeplechases, the fences are 4 ft 6 in (137 cm) high and over. In hurdle races, the fences are 3 ft 6 in (107 cm) high and over and are flexible, so that they bend if a horse hits them when jumping. In flat races, steeplechases, and hurdle races, Thoroughbred horses are used. This breed has been developed to have the strength and stamina to gallop fast over courses with or without jumps. In shorter flat races, horses may reach speeds of about 40 miles per hour (65 kilometers per hour). Harness racing requires a breed of horse that can pace or trot (see pp. 40-41) while pulling a sulky (a lightweight, two-wheeled cart). Breeds such as the Standardbred and the French Trotter have been developed especially for this type of racing. In pacing races the horses wear hobbles to prevent them from breaking into a gallop or trot. When racing, jockeys and drivers wear a set of silks, consisting of a jacket and cap in a particular pattern and color combination. Each racehorse owner has a specific pattern and color combination for his or her silks, so that the horse and its owner can be identified easily.

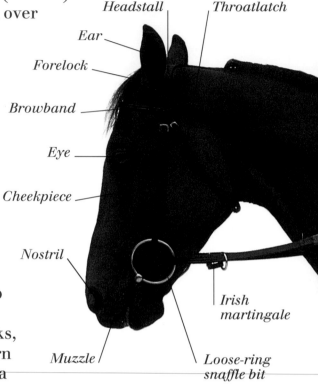

RACEHORSE AND JOCKEY

HARNESS RACING WITH A STANDARDBRED HORSE

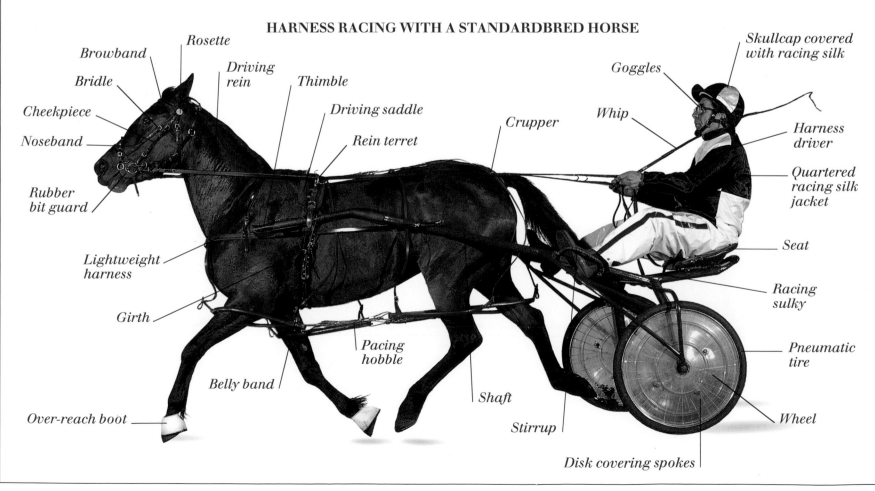

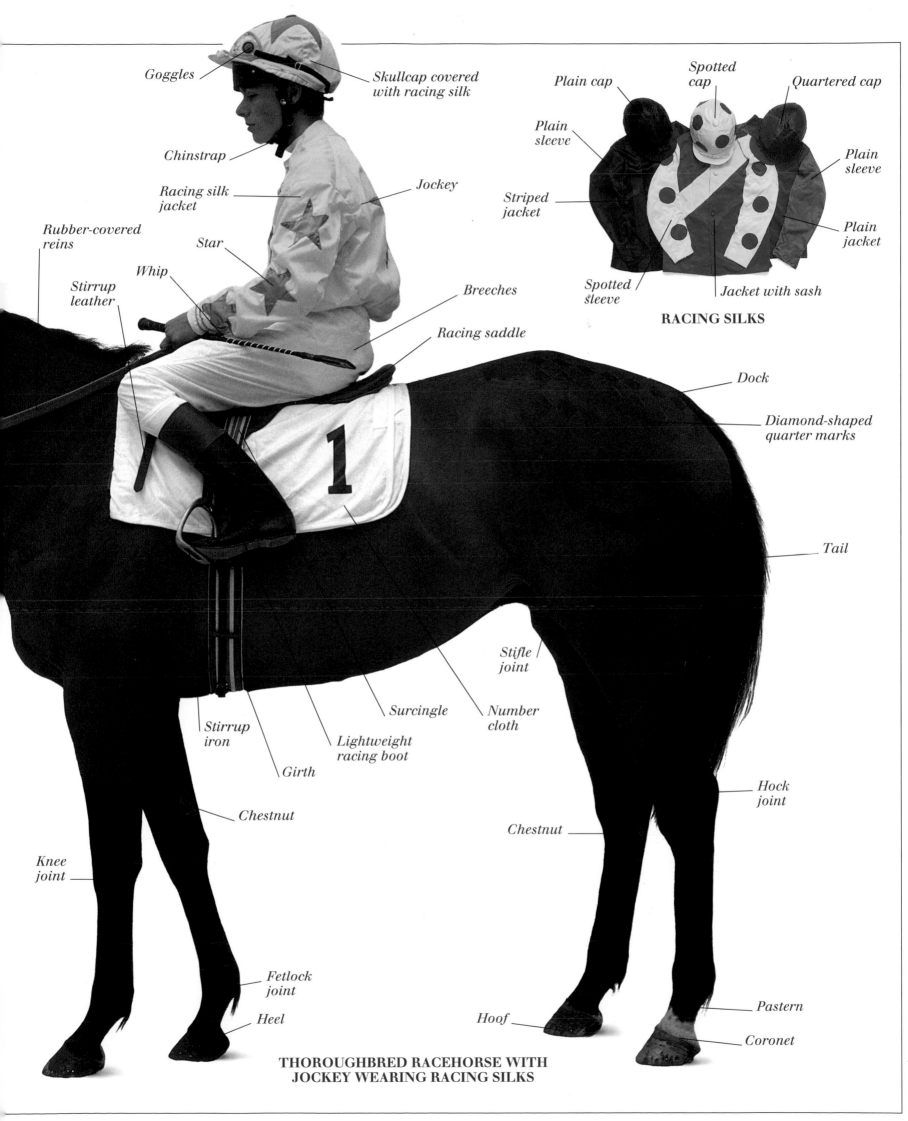

Goggles

Skullcap covered with racing silk

Chinstrap

Racing silk jacket

Jockey

RACING SILKS

Plain cap

Spotted cap

Quartered cap

Plain sleeve

Striped jacket

Plain sleeve

Spotted sleeve

Jacket with sash

Plain jacket

Rubber-covered reins

Star

Whip

Stirrup leather

Breeches

Racing saddle

Dock

Diamond-shaped quarter marks

Tail

Stifle joint

Surcingle

Number cloth

Stirrup iron

Lightweight racing boot

Girth

Chestnut

Hock joint

Chestnut

Knee joint

Fetlock joint

Heel

Hoof

Pastern

Coronet

**THOROUGHBRED RACEHORSE WITH
JOCKEY WEARING RACING SILKS**

Harnesses 1

HARNESS IS THE GENERAL TERM FOR THE EQUIPMENT that enables a horse to pull a load, such as a wagon, carriage, or plow. Most harnesses have three basic components: a bridle, collar, and breeching. The bridle is a set of straps that fits over the horse's head. Reins are attached to the bridle to enable the driver to control the horse. The collar is worn around the horse's neck or chest and is attached to the load by leather or chain traces. As the horse moves forward, it pushes against the collar to pull the load. The breeching is a set of one or more straps that fits on the horse's hindquarters. The most important component, called the breeching strap, fits behind the horse's hindquarters and enables it to brake or to reverse whatever it is pulling. There are many variations to these components, each adapted for a different function. For instance, bridles that are fitted with blinders—known as closed bridles—prevent horses from seeing anything approaching from behind or the sides, which could otherwise frighten them. Teams of two or more horses are harnessed in a different way from a horse working alone. For example, a pair of horses hitched to a wagon is usually positioned with one horse on each side of the wagon's central pole; each horse is attached by chains to the pole. However, a single horse pulling a wagon is usually hitched between two shafts, which are attached to the horse's collar by traces.

A PAIR OF SHIRES PULLING A DRAY

A PAIR OF SHIRES HARNESSED TO A PLOW

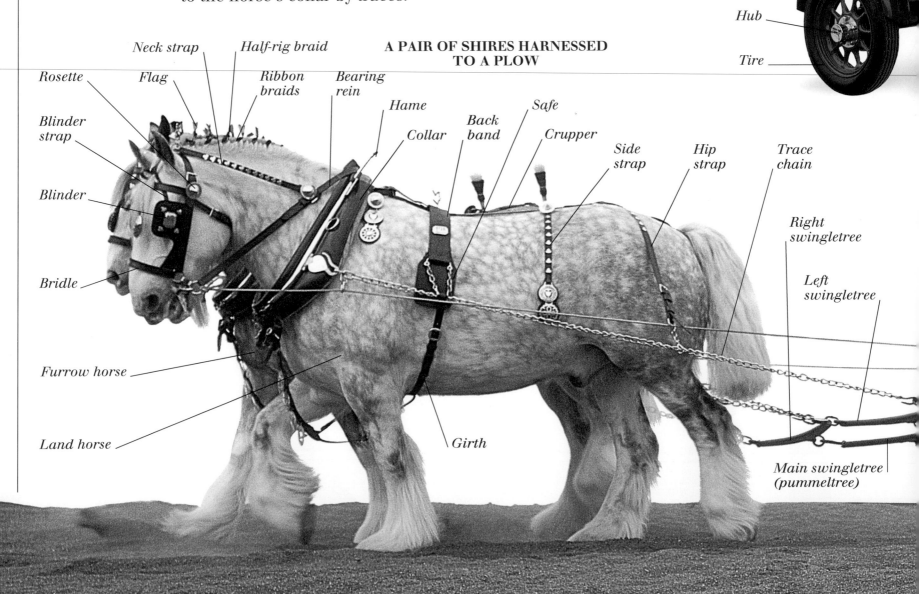

A PAIR OF SHIRES HARNESSED TO A DRAY

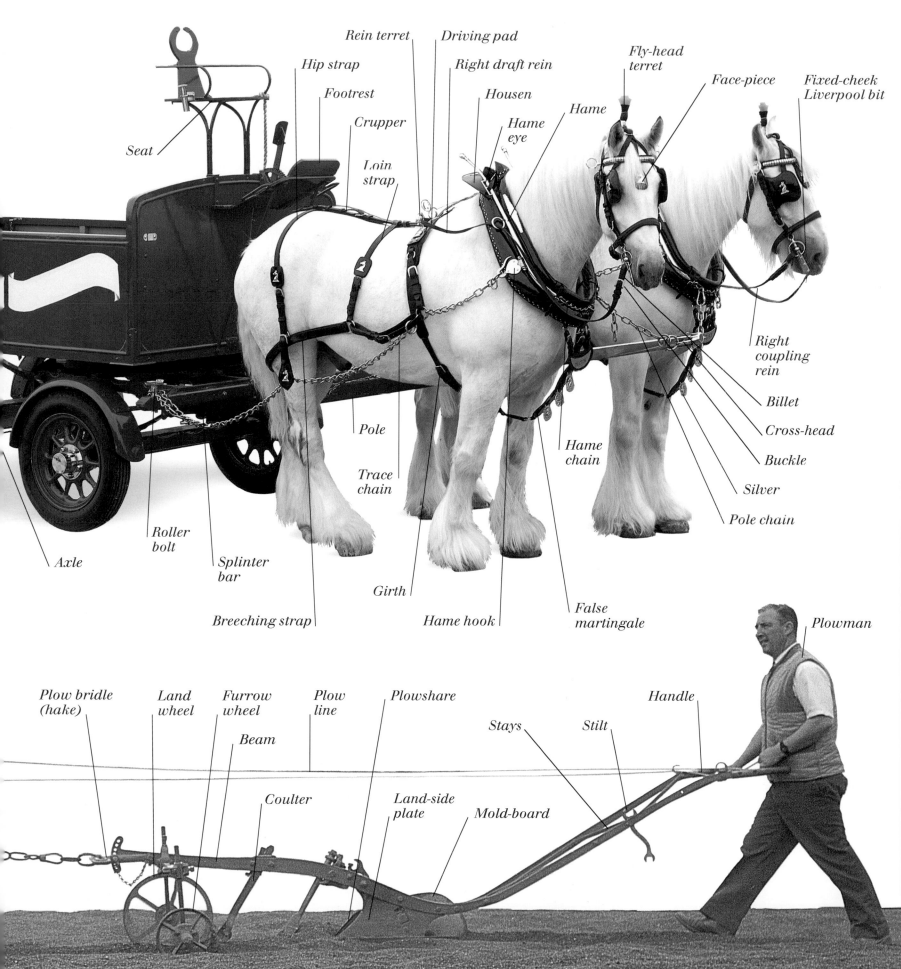

Rein terret

Driving pad

Hip strap

Right draft rein

Fly-head terret

Face-piece

Fixed-cheek Liverpool bit

Footrest

Housen

Crupper

Hame

Hame eye

Seat

Loin strap

Right coupling rein

Billet

Cross-head

Pole

Buckle

Hame chain

Trace chain

Silver

Roller bolt

Pole chain

Axle

Splinter bar

Girth

Hame hook

False martingale

Breeching strap

Plowman

Plow bridle (hake)

Land wheel

Furrow wheel

Plow line

Plowshare

Handle

Beam

Stays

Stilt

Coulter

Land-side plate

Mold-board

Harnesses 2

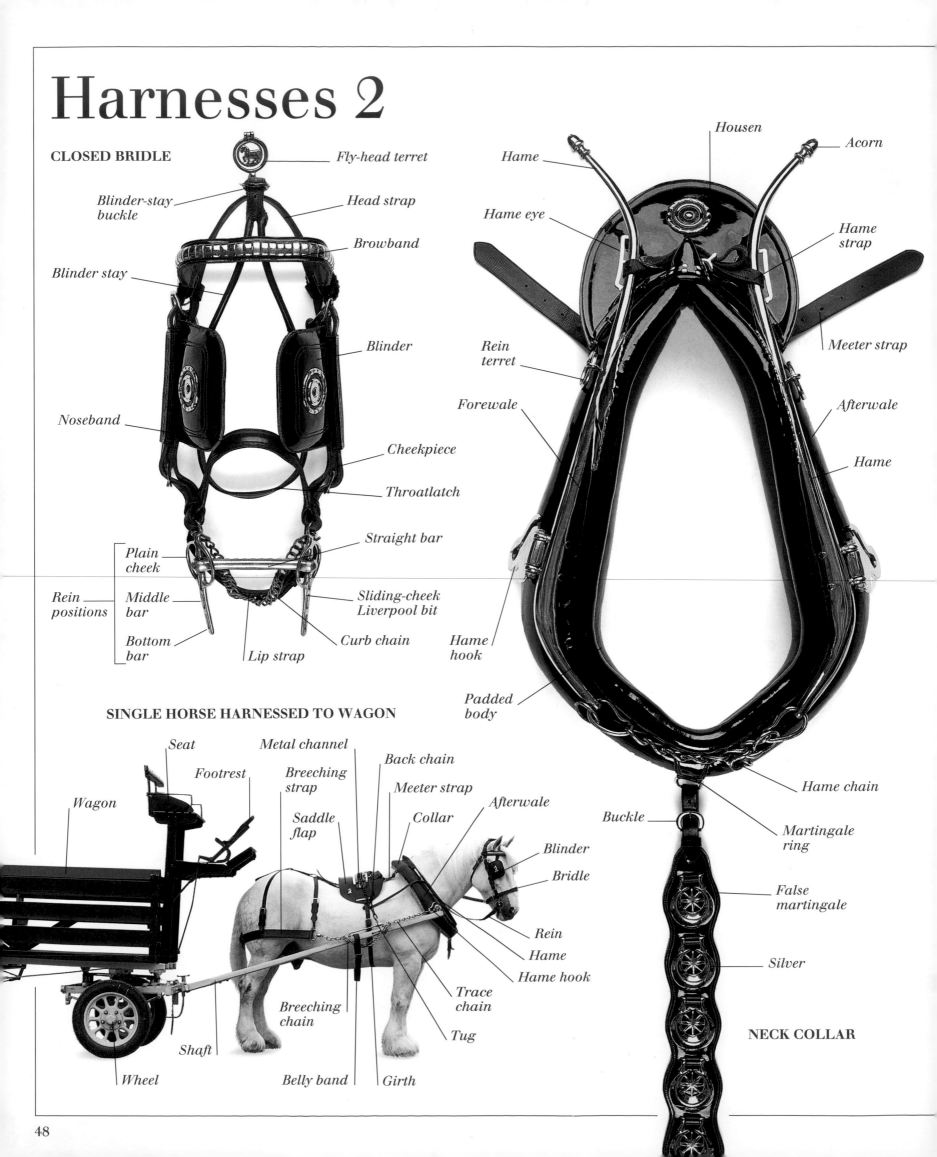

CLOSED BRIDLE

Fly-head terret

Blinder-stay buckle

Head strap

Browband

Blinder stay

Blinder

Noseband

Cheekpiece

Throatlatch

Straight bar

Plain cheek

Rein positions

Middle bar

Sliding-cheek Liverpool bit

Bottom bar

Curb chain

Lip strap

SINGLE HORSE HARNESSED TO WAGON

Seat

Metal channel

Back chain

Footrest

Breeching strap

Meeter strap

Wagon

Saddle flap

Collar

Afterwale

Blinder

Bridle

Rein

Hame

Hame hook

Trace chain

Breeching chain

Tug

Shaft

Belly band

Girth

Wheel

Housen

Acorn

Hame

Hame eye

Hame strap

Rein terret

Meeter strap

Forewale

Afterwale

Hame

Hame hook

Padded body

Hame chain

Buckle

Martingale ring

False martingale

Silver

NECK COLLAR

48

DRIVING SADDLE AND BREECHING

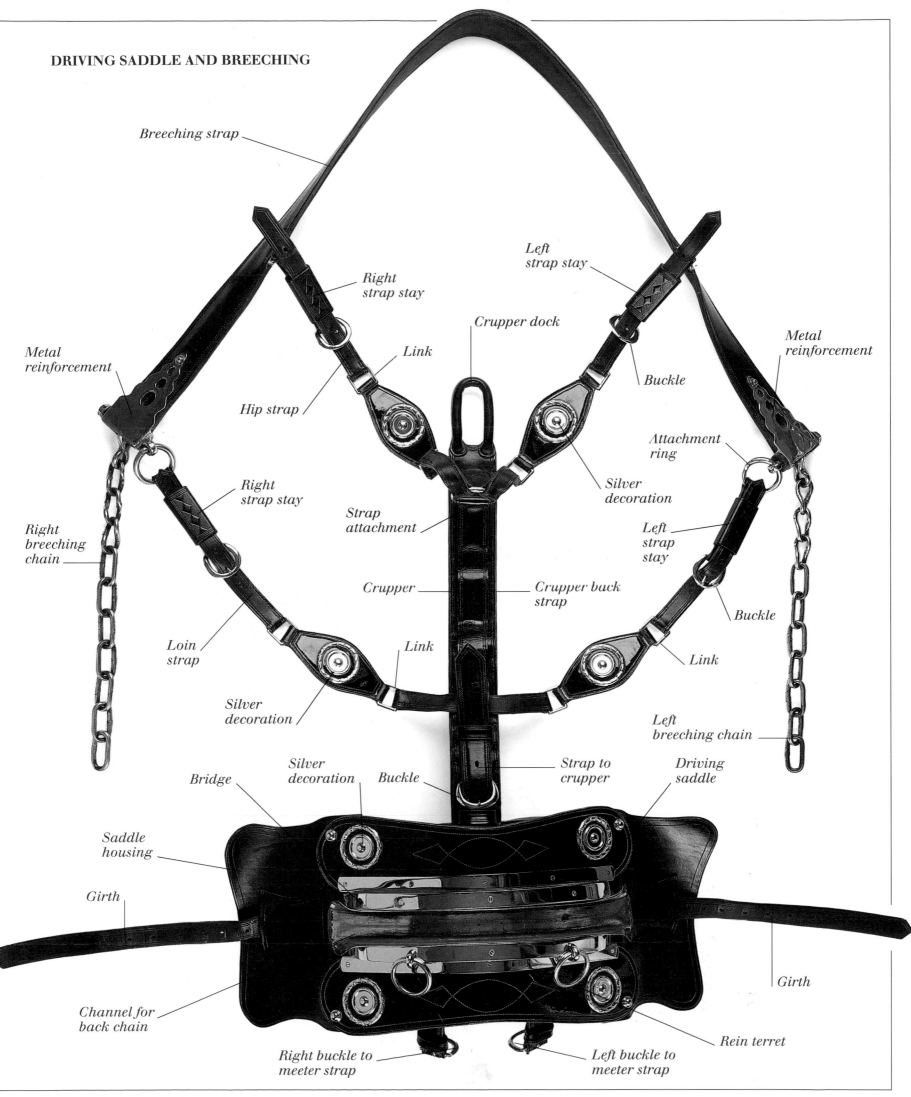

Breeching strap

Right strap stay

Left strap stay

Crupper dock

Metal reinforcement

Link

Hip strap

Buckle

Metal reinforcement

Right strap stay

Attachment ring

Silver decoration

Left strap stay

Strap attachment

Right breeching chain

Crupper

Crupper back strap

Buckle

Loin strap

Link

Link

Silver decoration

Left breeching chain

Silver decoration

Buckle

Strap to crupper

Driving saddle

Bridge

Saddle housing

Girth

Girth

Channel for back chain

Right buckle to meeter strap

Left buckle to meeter strap

Rein terret

Bits and bridles

BITS AND BRIDLES ARE USED TO REGULATE the position of the horse's head, and to help control the pace and direction of the horse. A bit is the part of the bridle that is fitted into the horse's mouth over the tongue. Most bits are made of metal (usually stainless steel), although the mouthpiece may be covered in rubber or vulcanite. The mouthpiece may be straight, mullen (half-moon), jointed, or ported (with a hump in the middle). Bridles typically consist of a headstall, and reins that are attached to the bit. There are various types of bridle, including double, snaffle, and Western bridles. The double bridle has two sets of reins and two bits—a curb bit and a snaffle bit (the snaffle bit is known as a bridoon when used in this way). The snaffle bridle has one set of reins attached to a snaffle bit. The Western bridle usually has one set of open-ended reins and a curb bit.

BRIDLING A HORSE

EXAMPLES OF BITS

Straight-bar mouthpiece

Cheekpiece ring

Rein ring

Curb chain

Rounding

Rein

Lip-strap buckle

Lip strap

Rein ring

STRAIGHT-BAR PELHAM

Mullen mouthpiece

Eggbutt ring for rein

EGGBUTT SNAFFLE

Cheekpiece ring

Rein ring

Rein ring

Curb chain

Mullen mouthpiece

MULLEN-MOUTH PELHAM

Double-jointed mouthpiece

Full cheek

Eggbutt ring for rein

Keys

BREAKING SNAFFLE

Cheekpiece ring

Ported mouthpiece

Cheekpiece

Rein ring

Rein ring

D-ring for rein

Curb chain

KIMBERWICKIE PELHAM

Jointed mouthpiece

GAG

Headstall

Noseband headstall

Bridoon sliphead

Browband

Throatlatch

Bridoon sliphead

Cavesson noseband

Curb cheekpiece

Ported mouthpiece

Bridoon (loose-ring snaffle bit)

Jointed mouthpiece

Lip-strap ring

Curb bit

Cheek

Rein ring

Curb chain

Fly link

Bridoon rein

Curb rein

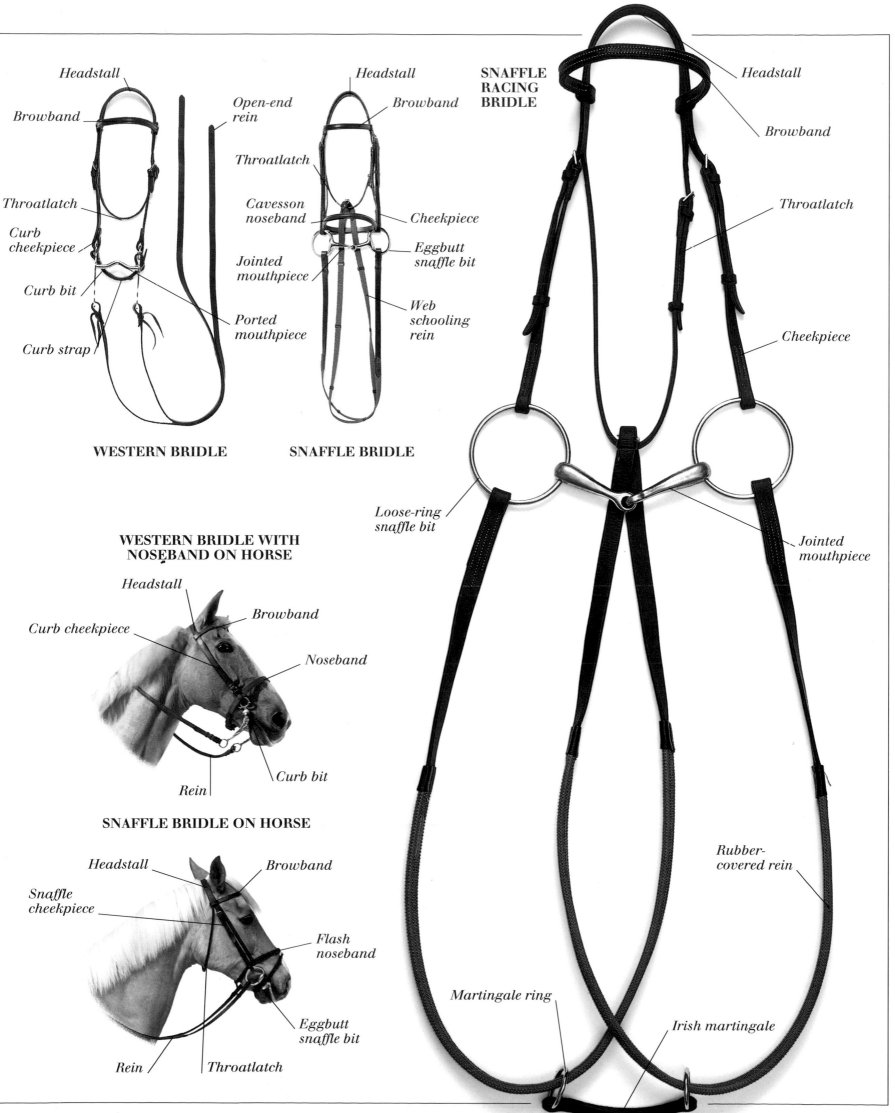

Headstall

Browband

Throatlatch

Curb cheekpiece

Curb bit

Curb strap

Open-end rein

Ported mouthpiece

WESTERN BRIDLE

Headstall

Browband

Throatlatch

Cavesson noseband

Jointed mouthpiece

Cheekpiece

Eggbutt snaffle bit

Web schooling rein

SNAFFLE BRIDLE

SNAFFLE RACING BRIDLE

Headstall

Browband

Throatlatch

Cheekpiece

Loose-ring snaffle bit

Jointed mouthpiece

WESTERN BRIDLE WITH NOSEBAND ON HORSE

Headstall

Curb cheekpiece

Browband

Noseband

Rein

Curb bit

SNAFFLE BRIDLE ON HORSE

Headstall

Snaffle cheekpiece

Browband

Flash noseband

Eggbutt snaffle bit

Rein

Throatlatch

Rubber-covered rein

Martingale ring

Irish martingale

51

Saddles

A SADDLE MAKES RIDING COMFORTABLE, as well as safer for both rider and horse. It enables the rider to sit on the horse securely and to move freely, and it also helps protect the horse. A saddle is built on a strong frame called a tree. On the underside of the saddle there is a channel called a gullet, which runs along the center and fits over the horse's spine to protect it. On each side of the gullet there is a padded panel that prevents pressure on the horse's spine. A saddle is held in position with a strap, known as a girth or cinch, which fits around the horse's barrel and is secured on each side of the saddle by buckles. Stirrups are also attached to the saddle to help the rider balance on and maneuver the horse. There are various types of saddle, each modified for a different type of riding. For example, a show jumping saddle has forward-cut flaps to help the rider sit in the correct position for jumping: leaning forward with the knees bent. A Western saddle is designed for riding for long periods; the saddle seat is padded and the stirrups are long so that the rider can sit in a relaxed position.

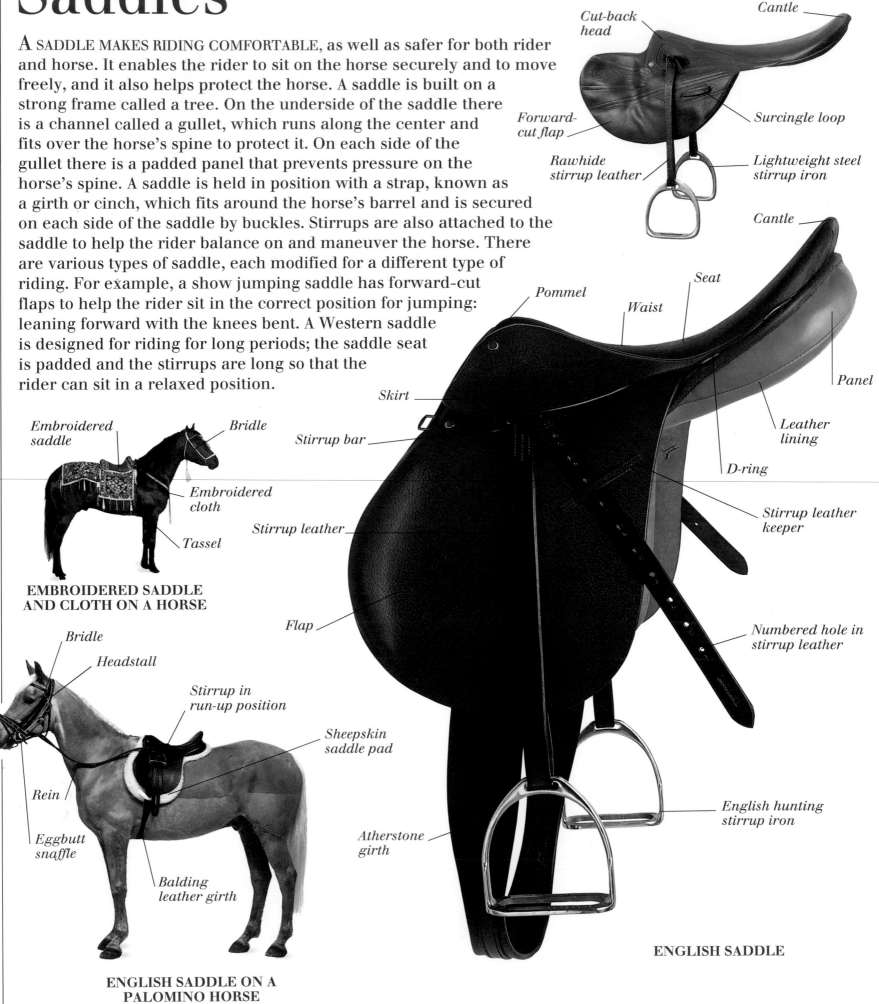

RACING SADDLE

Cut-back head

Cantle

Forward-cut flap

Surcingle loop

Rawhide stirrup leather

Lightweight steel stirrup iron

Embroidered saddle

Bridle

Embroidered cloth

Tassel

EMBROIDERED SADDLE AND CLOTH ON A HORSE

Pommel

Waist

Seat

Cantle

Panel

Skirt

Leather lining

Stirrup bar

D-ring

Stirrup leather

Stirrup leather keeper

Flap

Numbered hole in stirrup leather

Bridle

Headstall

Stirrup in run-up position

Sheepskin saddle pad

Rein

Eggbutt snaffle

Balding leather girth

Atherstone girth

English hunting stirrup iron

ENGLISH SADDLE

ENGLISH SADDLE ON A PALOMINO HORSE

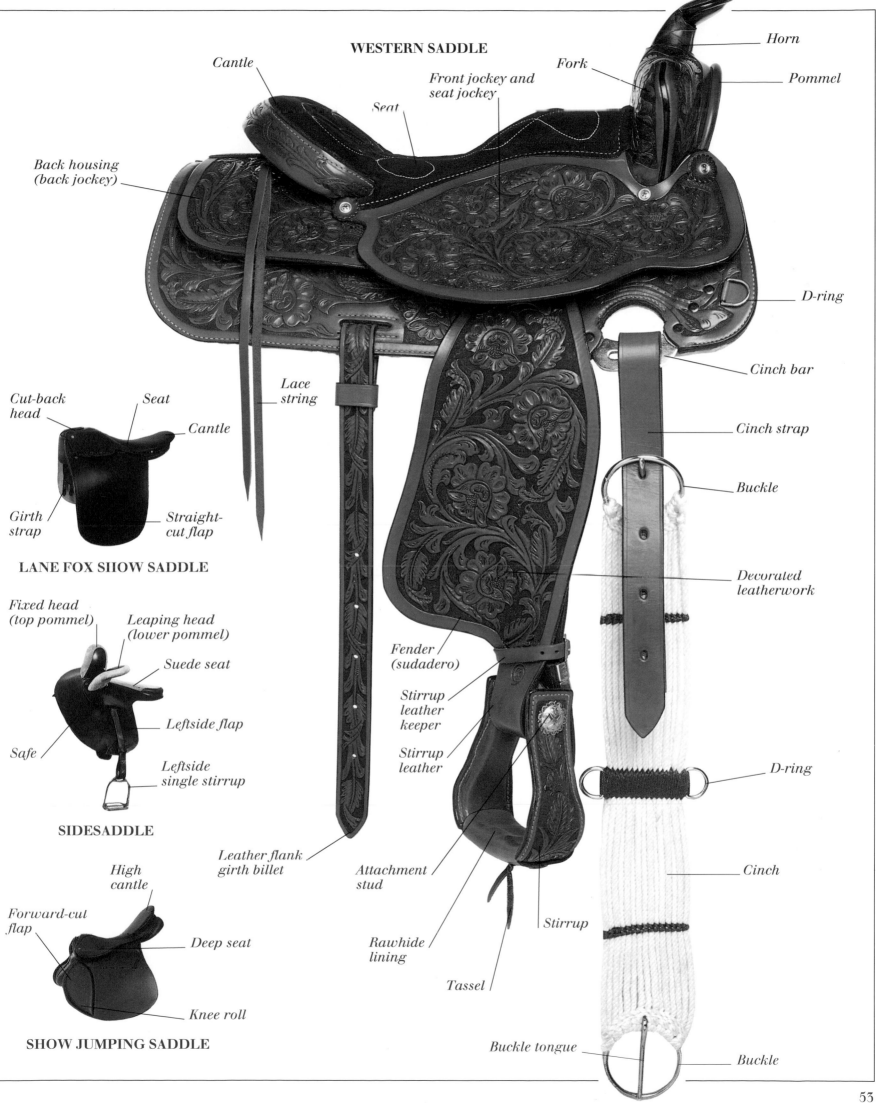

WESTERN SADDLE

Cantle

Seat

Front jockey and seat jockey

Fork

Horn

Pommel

Back housing (back jockey)

D-ring

Cinch bar

Lace string

Cinch strap

Buckle

Decorated leatherwork

Fender (sudadero)

Stirrup leather keeper

Stirrup leather

D-ring

Cinch

Leather flank girth billet

Attachment stud

Stirrup

Rawhide lining

Tassel

Buckle tongue

Buckle

LANE FOX SHOW SADDLE

Cut-back head

Seat

Cantle

Girth strap

Straight-cut flap

SIDESADDLE

Fixed head (top pommel)

Leaping head (lower pommel)

Suede seat

Leftside flap

Safe

Leftside single stirrup

SHOW JUMPING SADDLE

High cantle

Forward-cut flap

Deep seat

Knee roll

Grooming

GROOMING KEEPS THE HORSE'S COAT and hooves clean and helps to improve the circulation in the skin. During a grooming session, each part of the horse is carefully cleaned. Dirt and debris in the horse's hooves are picked out with a hoof pick, and the hooves may be oiled. If the horse is washed, excess water is scraped off its coat with a sweat scraper. If the horse is not washed, surface mud and sweat are brushed off the coat with a stiff-bristled dandy brush. Grease and dust are removed with a soft-bristled body brush that is cleaned every few strokes with a metal curry comb. Although the metal curry comb should never be used directly on the horse, the plastic curry comb can be brushed through the coat to remove mud, and a rubber curry comb used to remove mud and loose, shed hair. A soft cloth is used to give the coat a final wipe-down. The horse's eyes and nostrils are wiped clean with a damp sponge. The mane and tail are brushed thoroughly with a body brush or mane and tail comb. The mane may be damped down and brushed to one side with a water brush. If the horse is being groomed for a show, the mane and tail may be prepared for braiding with the mane comb. Patterns may be made on the horse's hindquarters by combing through a template in a different direction to the rest of the coat, creating quarter marks such as shark's teeth or a checkerboard. In winter, the horse grows a long coat, which may be clipped to prevent the horse from sweating excessively when being worked or ridden. The coat may be clipped entirely—a full clip—or only partly, as in the hunter clip for example.

BRAIDED MANE WITH FLAGS

QUARTER MARKS

Checkerboard pattern on hindquarters

Shark's teeth pattern on hindquarters

CHECKERBOARD

SHARK'S TEETH

EXAMPLES OF CLIPS

Unclipped area

Saddle patch left unclipped

Legs left unclipped

Legs left unclipped

CHASER CLIP

HUNTER CLIP

Brushing the horse from front to rear

Leather-backed body brush

Halter

BRUSHING THE HORSE

Jodhpurs

Metal curry comb for cleaning the brush

Rubber riding boots

GROOMING A HORSE

Cleaning the hoof with a hoof pick

PICKING OUT THE HOOF

Brushing oil on the hoof

OILING THE HOOVES

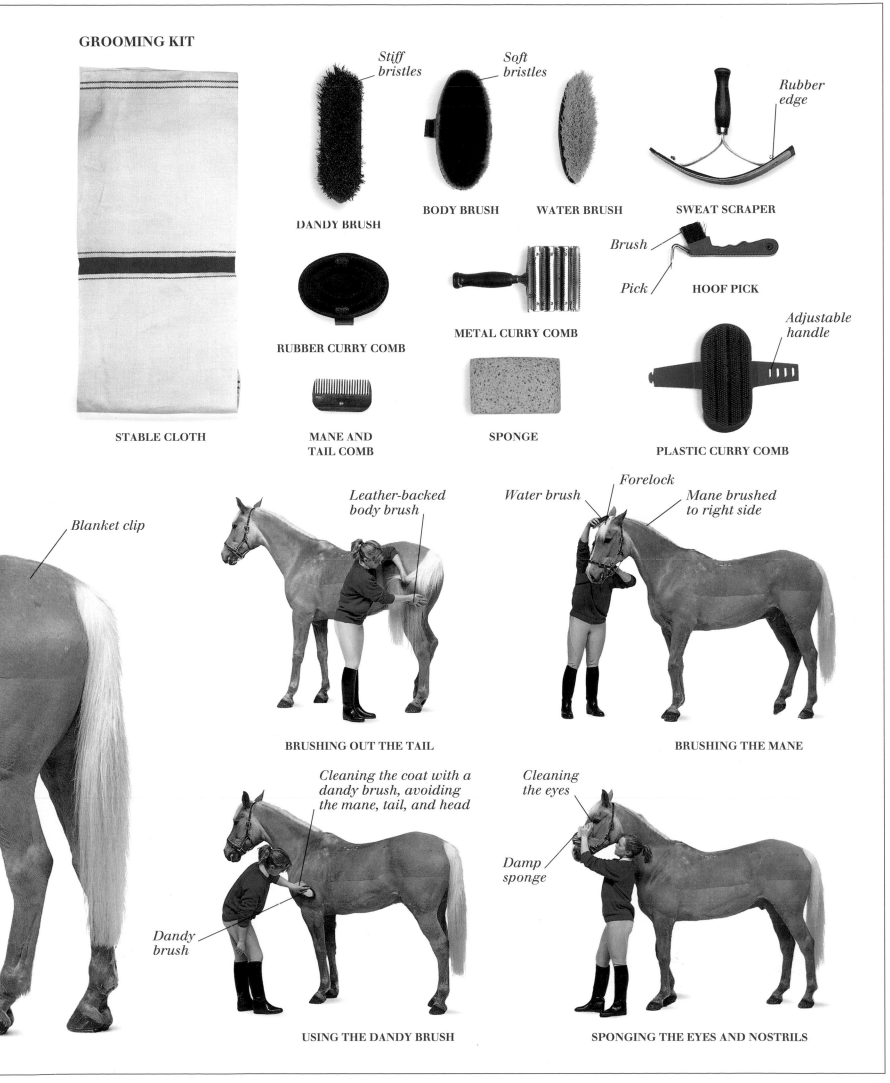

GROOMING KIT

Stiff bristles

Soft bristles

Rubber edge

DANDY BRUSH

BODY BRUSH

WATER BRUSH

SWEAT SCRAPER

Brush

Pick

HOOF PICK

RUBBER CURRY COMB

METAL CURRY COMB

Adjustable handle

STABLE CLOTH

MANE AND TAIL COMB

SPONGE

PLASTIC CURRY COMB

Blanket clip

Leather-backed body brush

Water brush

Forelock

Mane brushed to right side

BRUSHING OUT THE TAIL

BRUSHING THE MANE

Cleaning the coat with a dandy brush, avoiding the mane, tail, and head

Cleaning the eyes

Damp sponge

Dandy brush

USING THE DANDY BRUSH

SPONGING THE EYES AND NOSTRILS

Shoeing and shoes

A HORSE'S HOOF FORMS A PROTECTIVE COVERING over the sensitive inner part of the foot. Horses that are ridden or worked without shoes can wear down and damage their hooves, which may lead to sore feet or even lameness. To prevent injuries, horses are fitted with shoes by a farrier. The shoes are selected for particular functions; for instance, lightweight aluminum shoes (called racing plates) are worn for racing. To fit a new shoe, the farrier removes the old one and shapes the hoof with a rasp and a knife. The new shoe may then be fixed to the hoof by one of two methods: hot-shoeing or cold-shoeing. In hot-shoeing, the farrier shapes the shoe by heating it in a furnace until it is red-hot and malleable, then hammers the shoe into shape on an anvil. The farrier places the hot shoe on the hoof to burn a mark that acts as a guide for reshaping the shoe. The shoe is repeatedly reheated and reshaped until it fits properly, and then it is nailed to the hoof. The nail-ends are cinched off with a hammer-claw, and the remaining sharp nail-heads are hammered over to form clenches. Finally, the farrier files smooth the clenches with a rasp and trims the hoof. In cold-shoeing, a shoe of the right size is nailed to the hoof without having been repeatedly reheated and reshaped. Racing plates are usually fitted using this method.

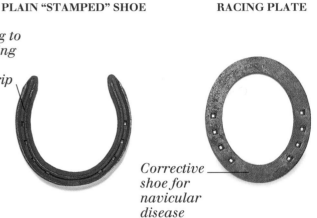

SHOES

Plain heel

Sturdy shoe for heavy horses

Lightweight aluminum shoe for racehorses

PLAIN "STAMPED" SHOE   RACING PLATE

Fullering to give riding horses better grip

Corrective shoe for navicular disease

FULLERED SHOE   "EGG-BAR" SURGICAL SHOE

Farrier files hoof to its normal length, after removing old shoe

Rasp

Hammer

Knife

PREPARING THE HOOF

HOT-SHOEING A HORSE

Furnace

Shoe is heated in furnace to make it malleable

Embers   *Tongs*   *Long-handled pincers*

FORGING (HEATING AND SHAPING) THE SHOE

Overgrown part of hoof is removed, and hoof is trimmed and cleaned

Knife

Hammer

Hammer

Anvil

TRIMMING THE HOOF

Shoe is hammered into shape

Tongs

SHAPING THE SHOE

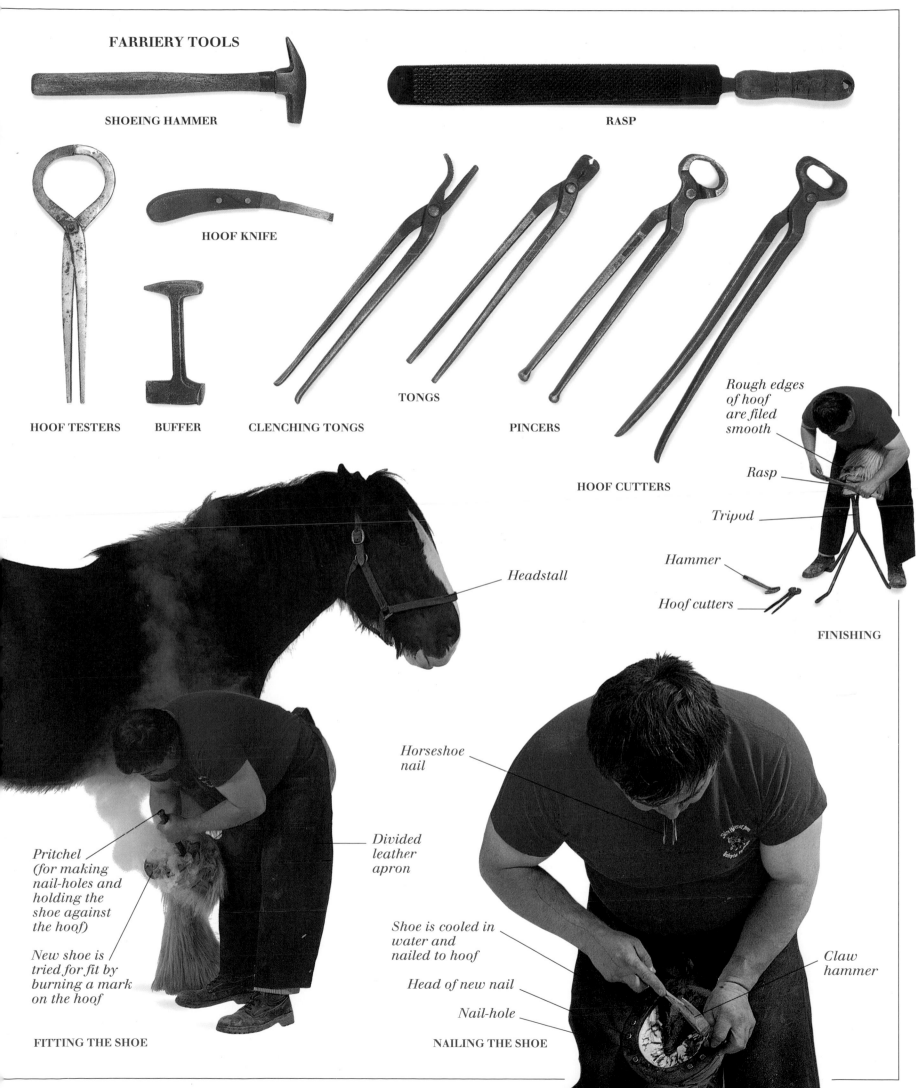

FARRIERY TOOLS

SHOEING HAMMER

RASP

HOOF KNIFE

HOOF TESTERS

BUFFER

CLENCHING TONGS

TONGS

PINCERS

HOOF CUTTERS

Rough edges of hoof are filed smooth

Rasp

Tripod

Hammer

Hoof cutters

FINISHING

Headstall

Pritchel (for making nail-holes and holding the shoe against the hoof)

New shoe is tried for fit by burning a mark on the hoof

Divided leather apron

FITTING THE SHOE

Horseshoe nail

Shoe is cooled in water and nailed to hoof

Head of new nail

Nail-hole

Claw hammer

NAILING THE SHOE

Horse family

HORSES, ASSES, AND ZEBRAS belong to a single family of mammals called the Equidae, the present-day members of which are shown below. The Equidae form part of a larger grouping called the Perissodactyla, which also includes rhinoceroses. Perissodactyls typically have either one or three digits on each limb; equids have one digit. In the wild, equids feed by grazing on grasses and shrubs, live in open country, and are fast-running animals that depend on speed to escape predators. They are highly social animals, living in large herds, each consisting of several family groups. All equids can interbreed to produce hybrids. For example, a male donkey mated with a female horse produces a mule. Most hybrids are sterile and therefore cannot have offspring.

EXAMPLES OF HYBRIDS

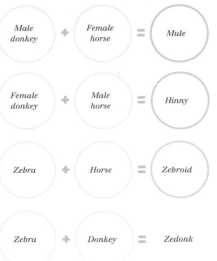

Male donkey + Female horse = Mule

Female donkey + Male horse = Hinny

Zebra + Horse = Zebroid

Zebra + Donkey = Zedonk

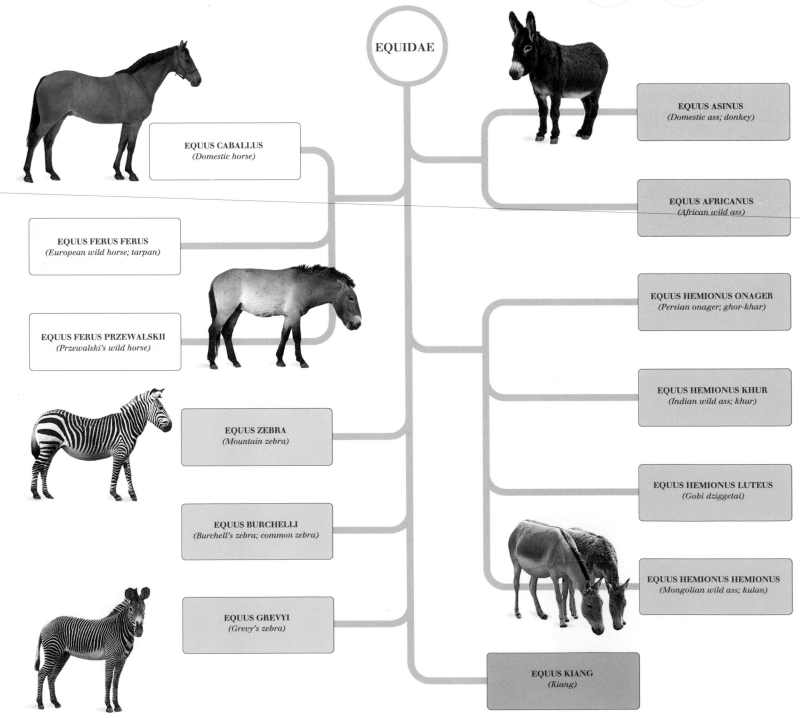

EQUIDAE

EQUUS CABALLUS
(Domestic horse)

EQUUS FERUS FERUS
(European wild horse; tarpan)

EQUUS FERUS PRZEWALSKII
(Przewalski's wild horse)

EQUUS ZEBRA
(Mountain zebra)

EQUUS BURCHELLI
(Burchell's zebra; common zebra)

EQUUS GREVYI
(Grevy's zebra)

EQUUS ASINUS
(Domestic ass; donkey)

EQUUS AFRICANUS
(African wild ass)

EQUUS HEMIONUS ONAGER
(Persian onager; ghor-khar)

EQUUS HEMIONUS KHUR
(Indian wild ass; khur)

EQUUS HEMIONUS LUTEUS
(Gobi dziggetai)

EQUUS HEMIONUS HEMIONUS
(Mongolian wild ass; kulan)

EQUUS KIANG
(Kiang)

Glossary

AGED: A horse that is seven or more years old.

AIDS: The means by which the rider or driver communicates his or her instructions to the horse. **Natural aids** include legs, hands, seat, and voice. **Artificial aids** include whips, spurs, and martingales. (See also Martingale.)

ASS: A member of the Equidae. The two existing groups of wild asses are the Asian wild ass and the African wild ass. (See also Equidae.)

BIT: The part of the bridle that is fitted into the horse's mouth over the tongue. Bits are made of metal, although the mouthpiece may be covered in rubber or vulcanite. The mouthpiece may be straight, mullen (half-moon), or ported (with a hump in the middle). There are various types of bits, including snaffle, pelham, and curb bits. (See also Bridle.)

BLINDERS: Leather flaps attached to the bridle, used to prevent a horse from seeing anywhere other than in front. (See also Bridle.)

BREAKING: The initial training of a horse for riding or harness work.

BREECHING: The part of a harness that enables a horse to brake or reverse when pulling a load.

BREED: An equine group that has been bred selectively for consistent characteristics over a long period of time. A true breed will be registered in a stud book. (See also Stud book.)

BRIDLE: The part of a horse's tack that is used to regulate the position of the horse's head, and to help control the pace and direction of the horse. There are various types of bridles, including double, snaffle, and Western bridles. (See also Tack.)

BRIDOON: A snaffle bit that is used with a curb bit on a double bridle. (See also Bit; Bridle.)

CANNON BONE: A bone in a horse's leg. In the foreleg the cannon bone is between the knee and the fetlock. In the hindleg the cannon bone is between the hock and the fetlock.

CANTER: One of the horse's natural gaits. It is faster than the walk and the trot, but slower than the gallop.

CHESTNUT: The horny, oval pad found on the inner side of the forelegs, and on the inner side of the hocks on the hindlegs. The term chestnut is also used to describe a reddish gold coat color.

COLLAR: The part of a harness that enables a horse to pull a load. The collar is oval, often made of wood, and covered in leather.

COLT: An ungelded male horse less than four years old. (See also Gelding.)

CONFORMATION: The overall external physical structure of a horse.

CRUPPER: A leather strap that helps keep the saddle or pad in place, preventing it from sliding forward.

DANDY BRUSH: A brush used to remove mud and sweat from a horse's coat.

DONKEY: A member of the Equidae. The donkey is a domesticated ass descended from the African wild ass. (See also Equidae.)

DORSAL STRIPE: A band of black hairs that extends along a horse's back.

EQUIDAE: A family of mammals consisting of horses, domesticated asses (donkeys), wild asses, and zebras.

ERGOT: A small, horny patch behind the fetlocks.

FARRIER: A person who makes horseshoes and shoes horses.

FEATHERING: Long hair on the lower part of the legs, particularly around the fetlocks. Heavy horses often have feathered legs. (See also Heavy horse.)

FILLY: A female horse less than four years old.

FLAT RACE: A horse race in which horses race over a track without jumps.

FOAL: A horse less than one year old.

FROG: The V-shaped, horny pad on the bottom of a horse's foot that acts as a shock absorber.

FULLERED SHOE: A horseshoe with a groove hollowed out along its surface. The groove makes the shoe lighter and gives the horse better grip.

GAIT (PACES): The way in which a horse moves. Most horses have four natural gaits: walk, trot, canter, and gallop. A horse can also be trained to do specialized gaits, such as pacing. (See also Canter; Gallop; Trot; Walk.)

GALLOP: The fastest of the horse's natural gaits.

GALVAYNE'S GROOVE: A groove that appears on the upper corner incisors and which can be used to determine the age of a horse.

GELDING: A castrated male horse. Stallions that are not suitable for stud purposes are often gelded to make them easier to manage.

GIRTH: The circumference of a horse, measured behind the withers and around the deepest part of the body. The term girth is also used for a strap that passes under the body to hold the saddle in place.

HALTER: A set of straps with lead rope attached, used for leading or tying a horse that is not wearing a bridle.

HAND: A unit of measurement used to describe a horse's height (which is measured from the highest point of the withers). One hand equals four inches (about 10 cm). Subdivisions of the hand are expressed in inches: thus 14.2 hands is 14 hands and 2 inches (58 in). (See also Withers.)

HARNESS: The equipment that enables a horse to pull a load. Harnesses usually consist of a bridle, collar, and breeching. (See also Breeching; Bridle; Collar.)

HEAVY HORSE: A large, powerful horse that has been used in agriculture and for hauling heavy loads. Heavy horses typically stand between 14.2 and 18 hands (58–72 in) high.

HINDQUARTERS: The part of the horse's body from the rear of the flank to the dock of the tail, as far down as the top of the gaskin on the hindlegs.

HINNY: The offspring of a male horse and a female donkey.

HURDLE RACE: A horse race in which horses race over a course with jumps that are 3 ft 6 in (107 cm) high and over.

LIGHT HORSE: Any horse, other than a heavy horse or pony, whose size and conformation make it suitable for riding or driving. Light horses typically stand between 14.2 and 17.2 hands (58–70 in) high.

MARE: A female horse more than four years old.

MARTINGALE: A strap, or set of straps, used to prevent the horse from lifting its head too high. The two most common types are the **running martingale** and the **standing martingale**. A third type of martingale, the **Irish martingale**, is used almost exclusively in racing to prevent the reins from flying over the horse's head in the event of a fall.

MULE: The offspring of a male donkey and a female horse.

NEAR SIDE: The left side of a horse. This is the side from which it is usual to mount and dismount as well as to lead the horse and to tack up. (See also Off side.)

OFF SIDE: The right side of a horse. (See also Near side.)

PEDIGREE: The record of ancestry of a horse. Pedigree must be proven in order to be entered into a breed society stud book. (See also Stud book.)

POINTS: The visible external features of a horse, such as the withers, as well as the parts of the skeleton and the superficial muscles that can be felt through the skin.

PONY: Any horse that is 14.2 hands (58 in) or less in height.

QUARTER MARKS: Decorative patterns on a horse's hindquarters made by brushing through a template in a direction different from the rest of the coat.

SADDLE PAD: A pad placed under the saddle to prevent undue pressure, rubbing, and chafing on the horse's back.

SILKS: The jacket and cap worn by a jockey in racing. Each set of silks has a particular pattern and color combination that are used to identify the horse's owner.

STALLION: An ungelded male horse more than four years old.

STEEPLECHASE: A horse race in which horses race over a course with jumps that are 4 ft 6 in (137 cm) high and over.

STIFLE: The joint between the lower end of the femur and the upper end of the tibia and fibula.

STIRRUP IRON: A loop, ring, or similar device suspended from a saddle to support the rider's foot. Stirrup irons are made of metal, usually stainless steel.

STUD BOOK: The book kept by a breed society in which the pedigrees of pure-bred stock are recorded.

SULKY: A lightweight, two-wheeled cart used in harness racing.

SURCINGLE: A belt that is used to keep a blanket or saddle in place.

SURGICAL SHOE: Any of various special types of shoe used to correct diseases or deformities of the hoof.

TACK: A general term covering all saddlery and harness equipment.

THROATLATCH: A leather strap that is a part of the bridle. The throatlatch passes around a horse's cheeks and under its throat. It helps to prevent the bridle from being pulled off over the horse's ears in the event of a fall. (See also Bridle.)

TROT: One of the horse's natural gaits. It is faster than the walk but slower than the canter and gallop.

TYPE: A horse that fulfills a specific purpose but does not necessarily belong to a specific breed. For example, a hunter is a riding horse that is used specifically for hunting. (See also Breed.)

WALK: The slowest of the horse's natural gaits.

WITHERS: The part of the horse at the base of the neck, where the neck joins the body, above the shoulders.

YEARLING: A horse of either sex, around the age of one year.

ZEBROID: The offspring of a zebra and a horse.

ZEDONK: The offspring of a zebra and a donkey.

Index

A

Abdominal oblique
  muscle 16-17
Accessory lobe 20
Accessory nerve 19
Acorn 48
Acoustic meatus 12
Adjustable handle 55
Adrenal medulla 19
Adult molar 14
Adult premolar 14
Adult teeth 14-15
African wild ass 58
Afterwale 48
Age 14
Aged 59
Agricultural work
  Heavy horse 36
  Pony 28
Aids 59
Air passage 20
Akhal-Teke 34
Alimentary tract 22
Allantoic cavity 26
Aluminum shoe 56
American Shetland pony 28
Amnion 26-27
Ampulla of vas deferens
  24-25
Andalusian 32, 35
Angle of mandible 12
Anglo-Arab 34
Anus 22-23
Anvil 56
Aorta 20-21, 24
Aortic valve 20
Apex 23
Aponeurosis of external
  abdominal oblique
  muscle 16
Appaloosa 9
Apron 57
Aqueous humor 18
Arabian 32, 34
Ardennais
  Colors and markings 9
  Heavy horse 39
Ariègeois pony 31
Artery
  Circulatory system 20-21
  Liver 23
  Urinary system 24
Artificial aids 59
Ass 59
  Horse family 58
Atherstone girth 52
Atlas 11
Atrioventricular valve 20
Atrium 20-21
Attachment ring 49
Attachment stud 53
Auditory meatus
  Ear 19
  Skull (side view) 12
Auricular muscle 17
Australian pony 28, 30-31
Axis 11
Axle 47
Azygos vein 21

B

Back 7
  Arabian 34
  Ardennais 39
  Australian pony 30-31
  Barb 34
  Bashkir 29
  Brabant 37
  Budonny 35
  Dales pony 29
  Dartmoor pony 29
  Don 35
  Dutch Draft 38
  Dutch Warmblood 35
  Exmoor pony 30
  Frederiksborg 32
  Haflinger pony 31
  Hanoverian 32-33
  Icelandic horse 30
  Italian Heavy Draft 37
  Kabardin 34
  Murakozer 38
  New Forest pony 28
  Nonius 35
  Norman Cob 37
  North Swedish horse 38
  Percheron 38-39
  Poitevin 38
  Russian Heavy Draft 38
  Shetland pony 29
  Shire 36-37
  Vladmir Heavy Draft 38
Back band 46
Back chain 48
Back fence 42
Back housing 53
Back jockey 53
Balding leather girth 52
Barb 32, 34
Bardigiano 28
Barrel 7, 52
Bashkir 29
Bay 8-9
Beam 47
Bearing rein 46
Belly 6
Belly band
  Harness racing 44
  Wagon harness 48
Biceps femoris muscle 16
Bile duct 23
Billet 47
Birth 26-27
Birth position 27
Bit 50-51, 59
  Closed bridle 48
  Dray harness 47
  Racehorse and jockey 44
Bit guard 44
Black 9
Bladder 24-25
Blanket clip 55
Blaze 8
Blinders 59
  Harness 46, 48
Blinder stay 48
Blinder-stay buckle 48
Blinder strap 46
Blood circulation 20-21
Blood vessel 20-21
Body
  Akhal-Teke 34
  Andalusian 35
  Anglo-Arab 34
  Arabian 34
  Australian pony 30-31
  Barb 34
  Caspian pony 31
  Cleveland Bay 32
  Dartmoor pony 29
  Exmoor pony 30
  Fell pony 30
  Foal development 26-27
  Frederiksborg 32
  French Trotter 35
  Hackney pony 31
  Haflinger pony 31
  Hanoverian 32-33
  Highland pony 29
  Icelandic horse 30
  Jutland 37
  Lipizzaner 32
  Morgan 33
  New Forest pony 28
  Norwegian Fjord 28-29
  Percheron 38-39
  Shagya Arabian 34
  Shetland pony 29
  Shire 36-37
  Suffolk Punch 36
  Tennessee Walking
  horse 33
  Tersk 35
  Welsh Mountain pony 30

Body brush 54-55
Body of cecum 23
Body of stomach 22
Body of uterus 25
Bones 10-11
  Ear 19
  Skull 12-13
Boot (horse)
  Harness racing 44
  Show jumping 43
Boot (rider)
  Grooming 54
  Racehorse and
  jockey 45
  Show jumping 43
Bottom bar 48
Boulonnais 37
Brabant 37
Brachial artery 21
Brachialis muscle 17
Brachial plexus 19
Brachial vein 21
Brachiocephalic artery 21
Brachiocephalicus
  muscle 17
Braided forelock 7
Braided mane
  External features 7
  Grooming 54
Brain
  Nervous system 18
  Skull 12
Brainstem 18
Breaking-in 59
Breaking snaffle 50
Breeches 45
Breeching 59
  Harness 46, 49
Breeching chain
  Driving saddle and
  breeching 49
  Wagon harness 48
Breeching strap
  Dray harness 47
  Driving saddle and
  breeching 49
  Harness 46
  Wagon harness 48
Breed 59
  External features 6
  Heavy horse 36-39
  Light horse 32-35
  Pony 28-31
Breton 37
Bridge 49
Bridle 50-51, 59
  Closed bridle 48
  Harness racing 44
  Plow harness 46
  Saddles 52
  Wagon harness 48
Bridling a horse 50
Bridoon 50, 59
Bridoon cheekpiece 50
Bridoon rein 50
Bridoon sliphead 50
Brisket 7
Bristles 54-55
Bronchus 20
Browband
  Bits and bridles 50-51
  Closed bridle 48
  Harness racing 44
  Show jumping 43
Brown 9
Brush 54-55
Brushing out the tail 54-55
Brushing the horse 54-55
Buccinator muscle 17
Buckle
  Harness 47, 48-49
  Saddle 52-53
Buckle to meeter strap 49
Buckle tongue 53
Budonny 35
Buffer 57
Bulb of penis 24
Bulbourethral gland 25
Burchell's zebra 58

C

Calcaneus 10
Camargue 9

Canine
  Skull (side view) 13
  Teeth 14-15
Cannon bone 59
  Arabian 34
  Australian pony 30-31
  Bashkir 29
  Boulonnais 37
  Dartmoor pony 29
  Dutch Warmblood 35
  Exmoor pony 30
  External features 6-7
  Foal development 26
  Hackney pony 31
  Haflinger pony 31
  Hanoverian 32-33
  Highland pony 29
  Icelandic horse 30
  Shire 36-37
  Skeleton 10-11
  Trakehner 35
Canter 59
  Gait 40-41
Cantle 52-53
Cap 45
Capillaries 20-21
Carbon dioxide 20
Cardiac gland region 22
Cardiac muscle 16
Cardiac opening 22
Carotid artery 21
Carpal extensor muscle 17
Carpal flexor muscle
  16-17
Carpal joint 7
Carpals 10-11
Carriage 46
Carriage horse 32
Cart 44
Caspian pony 28, 31
Categories 6
Caudal deep pectoral
  muscle 17
Caudal gluteal artery 20
Caudal mesenteric
  artery 20
Caudal mesenteric
  ganglion 19
Caudal mesenteric vein 20
Caudal vena cava
  Liver 23
  Respiratory and
  circulatory systems
  (side view) 21
Caudate process 23
Cavesson noseband 50-51
Cavity 12
Cecum 22-23
Cellulose 22
Cement 14-15
Central nervous system 18
Cephalic vein 21
Cerebellar fossa 12
Cerebellum 18-19
Cerebral crus 18
Cerebral gyrus 18
Cerebral sulcus 18
Cerebrum 18-19
Cervical rhomboideus
  muscle 17
Cervical sympathetic
  trunk 19
Cervical vertebra
  Skeleton 10-11
  Skull 12
Cervix 25
Channel for back chain 49
Characteristics
  Heavy horse 36
  Light horse 32
  Pony 28
Chaser clip 54
Checkerboard 54
Cheek (bridle part) 50
Cheek (external feature) 7
Cheekpiece
  Bits and bridles 50-51
  Closed bridle 48
  Harness racing 44
  Show jumping 43
Cheekpiece ring 50
Chest 7
  Ardennais 39
  Ariègeois pony 31
  Australian pony 30-31

Brabant 37
Breton 37
Clydesdale 36
Dartmoor pony 29
Exmoor pony 30
Haflinger pony 31
Italian Heavy Draft 37
Jutland 37
New Forest pony 28
Norman Cob 37
Norwegian Fjord 28-29
Percheron 38-39
Russian Heavy Draft 38
Shire 36-37
Suffolk Punch 36
Vladmir Heavy
  Draft 38
Chestnut (color) 59
  Colors and markings 8-9
Chestnut (external
  feature) 59
  Horse external features 7
  Racehorse and jockey 45
Chin 7
Chinstrap 45
Chordae tendineae 20
Chorion 26-27
Choroid 18
Cinch 52-53
Cinch bar 53
Cinch strap 53
Circulatory system 20-21
Claw hammer 57
Cleaning the brush 54
Clench 56
Clenching tongs 57
Cleveland Bay
  Colors and markings 9
  Light horse 32
Clip 54
Clitoral fossa 25
Closed bridle 46, 48
Clydesdale 36
Coat
  Appaloosa 9
  Ardennais 9
  Ariègeois pony 31
  Camargue 9
  Cleveland Bay 9
  Colors and markings 8-9
  Connemara 9
  Development and
  growth 26-27
  Frederiksborg 9, 32
  Friesian 9
  Grooming 54-55
  Heavy horse 36
  Holsteiner 9
  Lipizzaner 32
  Lusitano 9
  Norwegian Fjord 28-29
  Orlov Trotter 8
  Palomino 9
  Pinto 8
  Pony 28
Coccygeal vertebra
  Digestive system
  (side view) 23
  Skeleton 10
  Urinogenital system
  24-25
Coccygeus muscle 16
Cochlea 19
Coeliac artery 21
Coeliacomesenteric
  ganglion 19
Coffin (fence) 42
Coffin joint 10-11
Cold-shoeing 56
Collar 57
  Harness 46, 48
Collateral ulnar artery 21
Collateral ulnar vein 21
Colon 22-23
Colors 8-9
Colt 26, 59
Common carotid artery 21
Common digital artery 21
Common digital extensor
  muscle 17
Common digital extensor
  tendon 17
Common digital vein 21
Common zebra 58
Comtois 38

Conception 26
Condyle of mandible
  Adult teeth 15
  Skull (side view) 12
Conformation 59
  Heavy horse 36
  Light horse 32
  Pony 28
Conjunctiva 18
Connemara 9
Cooling the shoe 57
Copulation 24
Cornea 18
Coronary artery 20
Coronary venous
  plexus 20-21
Coronet
  Horse external
  features 6-7
  Racehorse and jockey 45
  Show jumping 43
Coronoid process of
  mandible
  Adult teeth 15
  Skull (side view) 13
Corpora nigra 18
Corpus cavernosum 24
Corpus spongiosum 24
Corrective shoe for
  navicular disease 56
Costal arch 23
Costal cartilage 11
Coulter 47
Coupling rein 47
Cranial cavity 12
Cranial gluteal artery 20
Cranial gluteal nerve 18
Cranial mesenteric
  artery 21
Cranial part of
  duodenum 22
Cranial superficial
  pectoral muscle 17
Cranial tibial artery 20
Cranial tibial muscle 16
Cranial tibial vein 20
Cranial vena cava 20-21
Cranium
  Foal development 26
  Skeleton 10-11
  Skull 12-13
Crest 7
Crest of ilium 25
Cross country fence 42
Cross country jumping 42
Cross-head 47
Cross poles 42
Croup
  Ariègeois pony 31
  Australian pony 30-31
  Barb 34
  Comtois 38
  Dartmoor pony 29
  Exmoor pony 30
  Foal development 26
  Haflinger pony 31
  Highland pony 29
  Horse external features 6
  Landais pony 31
  Murakozer 38
  New Forest pony 28
  North Swedish horse 38
  Norwegian Fjord 28-29
  Poitevin 38
  Shire 36-37
  Standardbred 33
  Vladmir Heavy
  Draft 38
  Welsh Mountain
  pony 30
Crown 14-15
Crupper 59
  Dray harness 47
  Driving saddle and
  breeching 49
  Harness racing 44
  Plow harness 46
Crupper back strap 49
Crupper dock 49
Cubital artery 21
Curb bit 50-51
Curb chain
  Bits and bridles 50
  Closed bridle 48
Curb cheekpiece 50-51

60

Curb rein 50
Curb strap 51
Curry comb 54-55
Curvature of stomach 22
Cut-back head 52-53

D

Dales pony 29
Dandy brush 59
  Grooming 54-55
Dapple-gray 8
Dartmoor pony 28-29
Decorated leatherwork 53
Deep digital flexor
  muscle 16-17
Deep digital flexor
  tendon 16
Deep pectoral muscle 17
Deltoideus muscle 17
Dental star 14
Dentine 14-15
Deoxygenated blood
  20-21
Depressor muscle 16
Developing umbilical
  cord 26
Development 26-27
  Teeth 14
Diamond-shaped quarter
  marks 45
Diaphragm
  Digestive system
  (side view) 22
  Respiratory and
  circulatory systems
  (side view) 21
Diastema 13
Digestion 22
Digestive juice 22
Digestive system 22-23
Digit 10-11
Digital artery 20-21
Digital extensor
  muscle 16-17
Digital extensor tendon
  16-17
Digital flexor muscle
  16-17
Digital flexor tendon
  16-17
Digital vein 20-21
Dilator muscle 17
Direction of blood flow 21
Disk covering spokes 44
Ditch 42
Divided leather apron 57
Dock
  Horse external
  features 6
  Racehorse and jockey 45
  Show jumping 43
Domestic ass 58
Domestic horse 58
Don 35
Donkey 59
  Horse family 58
Dorsal metacarpal
  artery 21
Dorsal metatarsal vein 20
Dorsal nasal meatus 12
Dorsal part of colon 23
Dorsal stripe 59
  Colors and markings 8
  Highland pony 29
  Norwegian Fjord 28-29
Dorsal turbinate bone 12
Double bridle 50
Double-jointed
  mouthpiece 50
Draft 37, 38
Draft rein 47
Drawing knife 57
Dray 46-47
Dray harness 46-47
D-ring 52-53
D-ring for rein 50
Driver 44
Driving pad 47
Driving rein 44
Driving saddle
  Driving saddle and
  breeching 49
  Harness racing 44

Driving saddle and
  breeching 49
Dun 8-9
Duodenal papilla 22
Duodenum 22
Dutch Draft 38
Dutch Warmblood 35

E

Ear
  American Shetland
  pony 28
  Ariègeois pony 31
  Caspian pony 31
  Dales pony 29
  Dartmoor pony 29
  Exmoor pony 30
  External features 7
  Fell pony 3
  Hackney pony 31
  Haflinger pony 31
  Highland pony 29
  Icelandic horse 30
  Landais pony 31
  Nervous system 18-19
  Norwegian Fjord 28-29
  Pottock pony 31
  Racehorse and jockey 44
  Shetland pony 29
  Welsh Mountain pony 30
  Welsh pony 29
Ear canal 19
Eardrum 19
"Egg-bar" surgical shoe 56
Eggbutt ring for rein 50
Eggbutt snaffle
  Bits 50-51
  English saddle 52
Elbow joint
  Horse external features 7
  Skeleton 11
Embroidered cloth 52
Embroidered saddle 52
Enamel 14-15
English hunting
  stirrup iron 52
English saddle 52
Entrance to stomach 22
Enzyme 22
Epididymis 24
Equid 58
Equidae 58
  Horse family 58
Equus
  africanus 58
  asinus 58
  burchelli 58
  caballus 58
  ferus ferus 58
  ferus przewalskii 58
  grevyi 58
  hemionus hemionus 58
  hemionus khur 58
  hemionus luteus 58
  hemionus onager 58
  kiang 58
  zebra 58
Ergot 6-7, 59
Erosion of central
  incisor 14
Erupting adult molar 14
Esophagus 22
Estrus 26
Ethmoturbinate bone 12
European wild horse 58
Eustachian tube 19
Eventing 42
Exit from stomach 22
Exmoor pony 30
Extensor muscle 16-17
Extensor tendon 16-17
External abdominal oblique
  muscle 16-17
External auditory meatus
  Ear 19
  Skull (side view) 12
External carotid artery 21
External features 6-7
External iliac artery 20
External iliac vein 20
External intercostal
  muscle 17
External jugular vein 21

External sex organs 27
External urethral orifice 24
Eye
  Exmoor pony 30
  External features 7
  Foal development 26
  Grooming 54-55
  Nervous system 18
  Racehorse and jockey 44
Eyelash 18
Eyelid 18

F

Face
  Colors and markings 8
  Foal development 26
  Pinto 8
Face-piece 47
Facial crest
  External features 6-7
  Skeleton (side view) 11
Facial markings 8
Facial nerve 18-19
Falabella 28
Fallopian tube 24-25
False martingale
  Dray harness 47
  Neck collar 48
False nostril 7
Family 58
Farrier 59
  Shoeing and shoes
  56-57
Farriery tools 57
Feathering 59
  Ardennais 39
  Boulonnais 37
  Brabant 37
  Clydesdale 36
  Dales pony 29
  Dartmoor pony 29
  Dutch Draft 38
  Heavy horse 36
  Highland pony 29
  Italian Heavy Draft 37
  Jutland 37
  Percheron 38-39
  Poitevin 38
  Russian Heavy Draft 38
  Shire 36-37
  Suffolk Punch 36
  Vladmir Heavy
  Draft 38
Feces 22
Fell pony 30
Female pelvis 25
Female urinogenital
  system 25
Femoral artery 20
Femoral fascia 16
Femoral nerve 18
Femoral vein 20
Femur 10
Fence
  Jumping 42-43
  Racing 44
Fender 53
Fertilization 24
Fetal membrane 27
Fetlock joint
  External features
  6-7
  Racehorse and
  jockey 45
  Show jumping 43
  Skeleton 10-11
Fetus 24, 26-27
Fibula 10-11
Filing the hoof 56-57
Filly 26, 59
Finishing 57
Fitting the shoe 57
Fixed cheek 50
Fixed-cheek Liverpool
  bit 47
Fixed head 53
Flag 46
Flank 6
Flap 52
Flash noseband 51
Flat-race 44-45, 59
Fleabitten gray 9
Flexor muscle 16-17

Flexor tendon
  Horse external
  features 6-7
  Muscles 16-17
Fly-head terret
  Closed bridle 48
  Dray harness 47
Fly link 50
Foal 59
  Development and
  growth 26-27
  Teeth 14
Food 22
Foot (fences) 42-43
Footrest
  Dray harness 47
  Wagon harness 48
Foramen magnum 12
Foramina 12
Forehead 7
  Australian pony 30-31
  Haflinger pony 31
  New Forest pony 28
  Percheron 38-39
  Russian Heavy Draft 38
  Suffolk Punch 36
Foreleg 7
Forelimbs
  Brabant 37
  Development and
  growth 27
  Italian Heavy Draft 37
  Percheron 38-39
  Shire 36-37
Forelock
  Grooming 55
  Head external features 7
  Racehorse and
  jockey 44
Forewale 48
Forging the shoe 56
Fork 53
Fornix 18
Forward-cut flap 52-53
Four-beat gait 40
Frederiksborg
  Colors and markings 9
  Light horse 32
French Trotter 35, 44
Friesian 8-9
Frog 59
Frontal bone
  Skeleton 11
  Skull 13
Frontal sinus 12
Front fence 42
Front jockey 53
Full clip 54
Fullered shoe 59
  Shoes 56
Fullering 56
Fundic gland region 22
Fundus 22
Furnace 56
Furrow harness 46
Furrow wheel 47

G

Gag 50
Gait 40-41, 59
Gallop 59
  Gait 40-41
Galvayne's groove 14, 59
Ganglion 19
Ganglionated sympathetic
  trunk 19
Gaskin
  Horse external
  features 6
  Show jumping 43
Gastric juice 22
Gelding 59
Germ of adult molar 14
Gestation period 26
Ghor-khar 58
Girth 59
  Dray harness 47
  Harness 48-49
  Plow harness 46
  Racing 44-45
  Saddles 52-53
  Show jumping 43
Girth strap 53

Gland 22
  Urinogenital system
  24-25
Glans penis 24
Gluteal artery 20
Gluteal fascia 16
Gluteal muscle 16
Gluteal nerve 18
Gobi dziggetai 58
Goggles 44-45
Gracilis muscle 16
Grass 22, 26
Gray 8-9
Great cardiac vein 20
Greater curvature of
  stomach 22
Grevy's zebra 58
Grooming 54-55
Grooming kit 55
Growth 26-27
Gullet 52
Gum 15

H

Hackney pony 31
Haflinger pony 31
Hair 26-27
Hake 47
Half-moon mouthpiece 50
Half-rig braid 46
Halter 54, 59
Hame
  Dray harness 47
  Neck collar 48
  Plow harness 46
  Wagon harness 48
Hame chain
  Dray harness 47
  Neck collar 48
Hame eye
  Dray harness 47
  Neck collar 48
Hame hook
  Dray harness 47
  Neck collar 48
  Wagon harness 48
Hame strap 48
Hammer 56-57
Hammer-claw 56
Hammering the shoe 56
Hamulus of pterygoid
  bone 12
Hand 6, 59
Handle 47
Hanoverian 32-33
Hard hat 43
Hard palate
  Adult teeth 15
  Skull section 12
Harness 46-49, 59
  Harness racing 44
Harness driver 44
Harness racing
  Gait 40
  Racing 44
Hauling a load
  Harness 46
  Heavy horse 36
Head
  American Shetland
  pony 28
  Bardigiano 28
  Dartmoor pony 29
  Development and
  growth 26-27
  External features 7
  Quarter horse 33
  Shetland pony 29
Headcollar
  Hot-shoeing 57
Headstall
  Bridle 50-51, 52
  Racehorse and jockey 44
Head strap 48
Heart 20
Heating the shoe 56
Heavy draft 37, 38
Heavy horse 6, 36-39, 59
Heel
  Horse external
  features 6-7
  Racehorse and jockey 45
  Show jumping 43

Height 6-7
Height range
  Heavy horse 6, 36
  Light horse 6, 32
  Pony 6, 28
  Racing fence 44
  Upright fence 42
Hepatic artery 23
Hepatic lymph node 23
Hepatic portal vein 21
Hepatic vein 21
Highland pony 29
Hindleg 6, 10
Hindquarters 59
  Akhal-Teke 34
  Andalusian 35
  Anglo-Arab 34
  Arabian 34
  Ardennais 39
  Barb 34
  Brabant 37
  Breton 37
  Budonny 35
  Cleveland Bay 32
  Clydesdale 36
  Comtois 38
  Dales pony 29
  Don 35
  Dutch Warmblood 35
  Frederiksborg 32
  French Trotter 35
  Horse external features 6
  Italian Heavy Draft 37
  Jutland 37
  Kabardin 34
  Lipizzaner 32
  Morgan 33
  Nonius 35
  Norman Cob 37
  Percheron 38-39
  Quarter horse 33
  Quarter marks 54
  Russian Heavy Draft 38
  Saddlebred 33
  Selle Français 35
  Shagya Arabian 34
  Shire 36-37
  Show jumping 43
  Standardbred 33
  Tennessee Walking
  horse 33
  Tersk 35
  Trakehner 35
  Welsh pony 29
Hinny 59
Hybrid 58
Hip joint
  Horse external
  features 6
  Skeleton (side view) 10
Hip strap
  Dray harness 47
  Driving saddle and
  breeching 49
  Plow harness 46
Hobble 44
Hock bone 10-11
Hock joint
  Horse external
  features 6
  Racehorse and
  jockey 45
  Show jumping 43
  Skeleton 10
Hog's back 42-43
Hole in stirrup-leather 52
Holsteiner 9
Hooded eye 30
Hoof
  Development and
  growth 26-27
  Grooming 54
  Horse external
  features 6-7
  Racehorse and
  jockey 45
  Shoeing and shoes 56-57
  Show jumping 43
Hoof cutters 57
Hoof knife 57
Hoof pick 54-55
Hoof testers 57
Horizontal ramus of
  mandible 13
Horn 53

Horn of uterus 25
Horse family **58**
Horse racing 44-45
Horseshoes 56-57
Horse types 6
Hot-shoeing 56-57
Housen
　Dray harness 47
　Neck collar 48
Humerus 11
Hunter clip 54
Hunting stirrup iron 52
Hurdle race 59
　Racing 44
Hybrid 58
Hyperglossal foramen 12
Hypoglossal nerve 18-19

I

Icelandic horse 30
Ileocecal fold 23
Ileum 23
Iliac artery 20
Iliac vein 20
Ilium 10-11
Incisive foramen 13
Incisor
　Digestive system
　　(side view) 22
　Skull 12-13
　Teeth 14-15
Incisor bow 13
Incus 19
Indian wild ass 58
Infraorbital foramen 13
Infundibulum 14-15
Intercostal muscle 17
Internal acoustic meatus 12
Internal carotid artery 21
Internal iliac artery 20
Internal iliac vein 20
Internal occipital
　protuberance 12
Involuntary muscle 16
Iris 18
Irish martingale 59
　Racehorse and jockey 44
　Snaffle racing bridle 51
Ischiatic nerve 18
Ischiocavernosus muscle 25
Ischium 10
Italian Heavy Draft 37

J

Jacket
　Racing 44-45
　Show jumping 43
Jaw
　External features 7
　Skull 12
　Teeth 14-15
Jockey (part of saddle) 53
Jockey (rider) 44-45
Jodhpurs
　Grooming 54
　Show jumping 43
Joint
　External features 6-7
　Hanoverian 32-33
　Skeleton 10-11
Jointed mouthpiece 50-51
Jugular foramen 12
Jugular groove 6-7
Jugular vein
　Muscles (side view) 17
　Respiratory and
　　circulatory system
　　(side view) 21
Jumping **42-43**
Jumping a parallel fence 42
Jump races 44
Jutland 37

K

Kabardin 34
Keys 50
Khur 58
Kiang 58
Kidney 24-25

Kimberwickie pelham 50
Knee joint
　Horse external features 7
　Racehorse and jockey 45
Knee roll 53
Kulan 58

L

Lace string 53
Lacrimal bone 13
Lacrimal fossa 13
Landais pony 31
Land horse 46
Land-side plate 47
Land wheel 47
Lane Fox show saddle 53
Lateral carpal flexor
　muscle 16-17
Lateral digital artery 20-21
Lateral digital extensor
　muscle 16-17
Lateral digital extensor
　tendon 16-17
Lateral digital vein 20-21
Lateral dorsal metacarpal
　artery 21
Lateral femoral fascia 16
Lateral nostril dilator
　muscle 17
Lateral palmar metacarpal
　artery 21
Lateral palmar metacarpal
　vein 21
Lateral palmar nerve 19
Lateral plantar metatarsal
　artery 20
Lateral plantar metatarsal
　vein 20
Lateral plantar nerve 18
Lateral splint bone 10
Latissimus dorsi muscle 17
Leading panel (fence) 43
Leaping head 53
Leather apron 57
Leather-backed body
　brush 54-55
Leather flank girth billet 53
Leather girth 52
Left atrioventricular
　valve 20
Left atrium 20-21
Left bronchus 20
Left coronary artery 20
Left foreleg 7
Left hindleg 6
Left horn of uterus 25
Left kidney 24
Left lobe
　Liver 23
　Lung 20
Leftside breeching
　chain 49
Leftside flap 53
Leftside single
　stirrup 53
Leftside strap stay 49
Leftside swingletree 46
Left ureter 24
Left ventricle 20-21
Legs 54
　American Shetland
　　pony 28
　Ardennais 39
　Australian pony 30-31
　Bardigiano 28
　Bashkir 29
　Boulonnais 37
　Brabant 37
　Breton 37
　Caspian pony 31
　Cleveland Bay 32
　Clydesdale 36
　Dales pony 29
　Dartmoor pony 29
　Dutch Draft 38
　Exmoor pony 30
　Fell pony 30
　Foal development 26-27
　Hackney pony 31
　Icelandic horse 30
　Italian Heavy Draft 37
　Jutland 37
　Kabardin 34

Landais pony 31
Lipizzaner 32
New Forest pony 28
Norman Cob 37
Norwegian Fjord 28-29
Percheron 38-39
Rocky Mountain pony 29
Russian Heavy Draft 38
Shetland pony 29
Shire 36-37
Skeleton 10
Suffolk Punch 36
Welsh pony 29
Lens 18
Leopard coat 9
Lesser curvature of
　stomach 22
Ligament of lens 18
Light horse 6, **32-35**, 59
Lightweight aluminum
　shoe 56
Lightweight harness 44
Lightweight riding boot 45
Lightweight steel
　stirrup iron 52
Lingual artery 21
Lingual vein 21
Linguofacial artery 21
Linguofacial vein 21
Lining 52-53
Link 49
Lip 7
Lipizzaner 32
Lip strap
　Closed bridle 48
　Straight-bar pelham 50
Lip-strap buckle 50
Lip-strap ring 50
Liver 22-23
Liverpool bit
　Closed bridle 48
　Dray harness 47
Lobe
　Liver 23
　Lung 20
Loins 6
Loin strap
　Dray harness 47
　Driving saddle and
　　breeching 49
Long digital extensor
　muscle 16-17
Long fixed cheek 50
Long-handled pincers 56
Long pastern bone 10-11
Loose-ring snaffle bit
　Bridle 50
　Racehorse and jockey 44
Lower canine 13
Lower eyelid 18
Lower incisor 12-13
Lower jaw
　External features 7
　Skull 12
　Teeth 14-15
Lower lip 7
Lower molar 15
Lower pommel 53
Lumbar vertebra
　Digestive system
　　(side view) 23
　Skeleton (side view) 10
　Urinogenital system 24-25
Lumbosacral plexus 19
Lung 20-21
Lusitano 9

M

Main swingletree 46
Major duodenal papilla 22
Male pelvis 25
Male urinogenital system 24
Malleus 19
Mandible
　Skeleton 10-11
　Skull 12
Mandibular foramen 12
Mane
　Andalusian 35
　Appaloosa 9
　Ardennais 9
　Ariègeois pony 31
　Bashkir 29

Camargue 9
Cleveland Bay 9
Color 8-9
Connemara 9
Dartmoor pony 29
Development and
　growth 26-27
Exmoor pony 30
External features 7
Fell pony 30
Frederiksborg 9
Friesian 9
Grooming 54-55
Haflinger pony 31
Holsteiner 9
Icelandic horse 30
Lusitano 9
New Forest pony 28
Norwegian Fjord 28-29
Orlov Trotter 8
Palomino 9
Percheron 38-39
Pinto 8
Rocky Mountain pony 29
Mane and tail comb 54-55
Mare 26-27, 59
Margo plicatus 22
Markings **8-9**
Martingale
　Dray harness 47
　Neck collar 48
　Racehorse and
　　jockey 44
　Show jumping 43
Martingale ring
　Neck collar 48
　Snaffle racing bridle 51
Masseter muscle 16-17
Mating 24, 26
Maxilla
　Skeleton (side view) 11
　Skull 12-13
　Teeth 14-15
Maxillary artery 21
Maxillary vein 21
Medial band 23
Medial digital artery 21
Medial digital vein 21
Medial dorsal metatarsal
　vein 20
Medial palmar nerve 19
Medial plantar artery 20
Medial plantar digital
　artery 20
Medial plantar digital
　vein 20
Medial plantar nerve 18
Medial splint bone 10-11
Median artery 21
Median nerve 19
Meeter strap 48
Mental foramen 13
Mesenteric artery 20-21
Mesenteric ganglion 19
Mesenteric vein 20-21
Metacarpal 10-11
Metacarpal artery 21
Metacarpal vein 21
Metal bit 50
Metal channel 48
Metal curry comb 54-55
Metal reinforcement 49
Metatarsal 10-11
Metatarsal artery 20
Metatarsal vein 20
Middle bar 48
Middle nasal meatus 12
Milk 26
Milk hair 26-27
Milk incisor 14
Milk premolar 14
Milk teeth 14
Minor duodenal
　papilla 22
Molar
　Digestive system
　　(side view) 22
　Skull (side view) 13
　Teeth 14-15
Molar bone 12
Mold-board 47
Mongolian wild ass 58
Morgan 33
Mountain zebra 58

Mouth
　Digestive system 22
　Foal development 26
Mouthpiece 50
Mudguard 46
Mule 59
　Hybrid 58
Mullen-mouth pelham 50
Mullen mouthpiece 50
Murakozer 38
Muscles **16-17**
　Heart 20
　Urinogenital system
　　24-25
Musculocutaneous nerve 19
Muzzle
　Australian pony 30-31
　External features 7
　Quarter horse 33
　Racehorse and jockey 44

N

Nail-ends 56
Nail-head 56-57
Nail-hole 57
Nailing the shoe 57
Nail pullers 57
Nasal bone
　External features 7
　Skeleton 11
　Skull 12-13
Nasal cavity 13
Nasal muscle 17
Nasal passage 20-21
Nasal peak 12-13
Nasal process of
　premaxilla 12-13
Nasomaxillary notch 12
Natural aids 59
Natural gait 40
Nearside 59
Neck
　Akhal-Teke 34
　Andalusian 35
　Ardennais 39
　Australian pony 30-31
　Barb 34
　Bardigiano 28
　Bashkir 29
　Boulonnais 37
　Brabant 37
　Breton 37
　Cleveland Bay 32
　Clydesdale 36
　Comtois 35
　Dales pony 29
　Dartmoor pony 29
　Dutch Draft 38
　Foal development 7
　Frederiksborg 32
　French Trotter 35
　Hanoverian 32-33
　Highland pony 29
　Horse external
　　features 7
　Italian Heavy Draft 37
　Jutland 37
　Kabardin 34
　Lipizzaner 32
　Murakozer 38
　New Forest pony 28
　Norman Cob 37
　North Swedish horse 38
　Percheron 38-39
　Poitevin 38
　Pottock pony 31
　Quarter horse 33
　Rocky Mountain pony 29
　Russian Heavy Draft 38
　Saddlebred 33
　Selle Français 35
　Shetland pony 29
　Shire 36-37
　Suffolk Punch 36
　Vladmir Heavy
　　Draft 38
　Welsh pony 29
Neck bone 12
Neck collar 48
Neck strap 46
Nerve 18-19
Nervous system **18-19**

New Forest pony 28
Nonglandular region
　of stomach 22
Nonius 35
Norman Cob 37
North Swedish horse 38
Norwegian Fjord 28-29
Noseband
　Bits and bridles 51
　Closed bridle 48
　Harness racing 44
　Show jumping 43
Noseband headstall 50
Nostril
　Australian pony 30-31
　Exmoor pony 30
　External features 7
　Foal development 26
　Grooming 54-55
　Haflinger pony 31
　New Forest pony 28
　Norwegian Fjord 28-29
　Percheron 38-39
　Racehorse and jockey 44
Nostril dilator muscle 17
Nuchal crest 12-13
Number cloth 45
Numbered hole in
　stirrup leather 52

O

Oblique carpal extensor
　muscle 17
Oblique muscle 16-17
Obturator nerve 18
Occipital artery 21
Occipital condyle
　Adult teeth 15
　Skull (side view) 12
Occipital protuberance 12
Oculomotor nerve 18-19
Offside 59
Oiling the hooves 54
Olecranon 11
Olfactory bulb 18-19
Open-end rein 51
Optic disk 18
Optic nerve 18-19
Optic tract 18
Orbicularis oris muscle 17
Orbit
　Adult teeth 15
　Skeleton 10-11
　Skull 12-13
Orlov Trotter 8
Ovary 24
Over-reach boot 44
Ovum 24
Oxer 42-43
Oxygen 20
Oxygenated blood 20-21

P

Pace 40-41, 59
Pacing 40
Pacing hobble 44
Pacing race 44
Pack animals 28
Palate 12
Palatine bone 15
Palatine sinus 12
Palmar metacarpal artery 21
Palmar metacarpal vein 21
Palmar nerve 19
Palomino 8-9, 52
Panel 52
Papillary muscle 20
Paramastoid process
　Adult teeth 15
　Skull 12
Parietal bone 12-13
Passages 12
Pastern
　Horse external
　　features 6-7
　Racehorse and
　　jockey 45
　Show jumping 43
Pastern bone 10-11
Pastern joint 10-11
Patella 10

Pectinate muscles 20
Pectoral muscle 17
Pectoral nerve 19
Pedal bone 10-11
Pedigree 59
Pelham 50
Pelvis 25
Penis 24-25
Percheron 36, 39
Peripheral nervous
  system 18
Perissodactyl 58
Perissodactyla 58
Permanent teeth 14-15
Peroneal nerve 18
Persian onager 58
Phrenic nerve 19
Pick 55
Picking out the feet 54
Pillar (fence) 43
Pincers 57
Pinna 19
Pinto 8
Pisiform 11
Pituitary 18
Plain cap 45
Plain "stamped" shoe 56
Plank 43
Plantar artery 20
Plantar digital artery 20
Plantar digital vein 20
Plantar metatarsal
  artery 20
Plantar metatarsal
  vein 20
Plantar nerve 18
Plastic curry comb 54-55
Plow 46
Plow bridle 47
Plow harness 46-47
Plowing 36
Plow line 47
Plowman 47
Plowshare 47
Pneumatic tire 44
Point of croup 25
Point of elbow
  Horse external features 7
  Skeleton (side view) 11
Point of hip
  Horse external features 6
  Pelvis 25
  Skeleton (side view) 10
Point of hock
  Horse external
  features 6
  Skeleton (side view) 10
Point of shoulder 7
Points 6, 59
  Heavy horse 36-39
  Light horse 32-35
  Ponies 28-31
Poitevin 38
Pole chain 47
Pole (part of fence)
  42-43
Pole (part of wagon)
  46-47
Poll 7
Pommel 52-53
Pony 6, 28-31, 59
Popliteal artery 20
Popliteus muscle 16
Portal vein 23
Ported mouthpiece 50-51
Position of rider
  Gait 40-41
  Jumping an oxer 42
  Saddle 52
Post 42
Pottock pony 31
Premaxilla
  Skeleton (side view) 11
  Skull 12-13
  Teeth 14-15
Premolar
  Digestive system
  (side view) 22
  Skull 13
  Teeth 14-15
Preparing the hoof 56
Prepuce 24
Preputial orifice 24
Pritchel 57
Process of frontal bone 13

Process of mandible
  Adult teeth 15
  Skull (side view) 13
Process of premaxilla 12-13
Profile
  Arabian 34
  Australian pony 30-31
  Boulonnais 37
  Breton 37
  Clydesdale 36
  New Forest pony 28
  Norwegian Fjord 28-29
  Percheron 38-39
Prostate gland 24-25
Proximal sesamoid
  bone 10-11
Przewalski's wild horse 58
Pterygoid bone 12
Pubic symphysis
  Digestive system
  (side view) 23
  Urinogenital system 24-25
Pubis 10
Pudendal nerve 18
Pulling a load
  Harness 46
  Heavy horse 36
Pulmonary artery 21
Pulmonary trunk 20
Pulmonary vein 20-21
Pummeltree 46
Pupil 18
Pyloric gland region 22
Pylorus 22

Q

Quadrate lobe 23
Quartered cap 45
Quartered racing silk
  jacket 44
Quarter horse 33
Quarter marks 59
  Grooming 54
  Racehorse and jockey 45

R

Racehorse 44-45
Racehorse and jockey
  44-45
Racing 44-45
Racing plate 56
Racing saddle
  Racehorse and
  jockey 45
  Saddles 52
Racing silk jacket 44-45
Racing silks 44-45
Racing sulky 44
Radial carpal extensor
  muscle 17
Radial carpal flexor
  muscle 17
Radial nerve 19
Radius 10-11
Ramus of mandible 12-13
Rasp 56-57
Rawhide lining 53
Rawhide stirrup leather 52
Rectum 22-23
Red roan 9
Reflex actions 18
Rein
  Bits and bridles 50-51
  English saddle 52
  Harness 46
  Harness racing 44
  Show jumping 43
  Wagon harness 48
Rein positions 48
Rein ring 50
Rein terret
  Dray harness 47
  Driving saddle and
  breeching 49
  Harness racing 44
  Neck collar 48
Renal artery 24
Renal vein 24
Reproductive organs 24
Respiratory system 20-21
Retina 18

Retractor penis
  muscle 24-25
Rhomboideus muscle 17
Rib
  Digestive system
  (side view) 23
  Skeleton 10-11
Ribbon braids 46
Rider's position
  Gait 40-41
  Jumping an oxer 42
  Saddle 52
Riding boot
  Grooming 54
  Racehorse and jockey 45
  Show jumping 43
Riding horse 32
Riding jacket 43
Riding pony 28
Right atrioventricular
  valve 20
Right atrium 20-21
Right breeching chain 49
Right bronchus 20
Right coronary artery 20
Right coupling rein 47
Right draft rein 47
Right foreleg 7
Right hindleg 6
Right horn of uterus 25
Right kidney 24-25
Right lobe
  Liver 23
  Lung 20
Right ovary 25
Right strap stay 49
Right swingletree 46
Right testis 24
Right ureter 24
Right ventricle 20-21
Rocky Mountain pony 29
Roller bolt 47
Root 14-15
Root of accessory nerve 18
Rope binding 42
Rosette
  Harness racing 44
  Plow harness 46
Rounding 50
Rubber (grooming) 54-55
Rubber bit-guard 44
Rubber-covered
  mouthpiece 50
Rubber-covered rein
  Racehorse and jockey 45
  Snaffle racing bridle 51
Rubber curry comb 54-55
Rubber edge 55
Rubber riding boot 54
Running martingale 59
  Show jumping 43
Russian Heavy Draft 38
Rustic upright with
  cross poles 42

S

Sacrum
  Digestive system
  (side view) 23
  Skeleton (side view) 10
  Urinogenital system 24-25
Saddle 52-53
  Driving saddle and
  breeching 49
  Harness racing 44
  Racehorse and jockey 45
  Show jumping 43
Saddlebred 33
Saddle flap 48
Saddle housing 49
Saddle pad 59
  English saddle 52
  Show jumping 43
Saddle patch 54
Safe
  Plow harness 46
  Sidesaddle 53
Saliva 22
Saphenous artery 20
Saphenous vein 20
Scapula 11
Scapular spine 11
Sciatic nerve 18

Sclera 18
Scraper 54-55
Scrotum 24
Season 24, 26
Seat
  Dray harness 47
  Harness racing 44
  Saddle 52-53
  Wagon harness 48
Seat jockey 53
Selective breeding 6
Selle Français 35
Semicircular canal 19
Semimembranosus
  muscle 16
Semitendinosus muscle 16
Sensory organ 18
Septomarginal trabecula 20
Serratus muscle 17
Sesamoid bone 10-11
Sex cells 24
Sex organs 27
Sexual maturity 24, 26
Shaft
  Harness 46
  Harness racing 44
  Wagon harness 48
Shagya Arabian 34
Shaping the hoof 56
Shaping the shoe 56
Shark's teeth 54
Sheath 24
Sheepskin saddle pad
  English saddle 52
  Show jumping 43
Shetland pony 29
Shire 36-37
  Harness 46-47
  Shire mare and
  foal 26
Shoe 56-57
Shoeing 56-57
Shoeing hammer 57
Short pastern bone
  10-11
Shoulder
  Akhal-Teke 34
  American Shetland
  pony 28
  Andalusian 35
  Anglo-Arab 34
  Arabian 34
  Australian pony 30-31
  Barb 34
  Bardigiano 28
  Bashkir 29
  Boulonnais 37
  Budonny 35
  Caspian pony 31
  Cleveland Bay 32
  Comtois 38
  Dales pony 29
  Dartmoor pony 29
  Don 35
  Dutch Draft 38
  Dutch Warmblood 35
  Fell pony 30
  Frederiksborg 32
  French Trotter 35
  Hackney pony 31
  Hanoverian 32-33
  Horse external
  features 7
  Kabardin 34
  Landais pony 31
  Morgan 33
  Murakozer 38
  New Forest pony 28
  Nonius 35
  North Swedish horse 38
  Percheron 38-39
  Pottock pony 31
  Quarter horse 33
  Russian Heavy
  Draft 38
  Saddlebred 33
  Selle Français 35
  Shagya Arabian 34
  Shetland pony 29
  Shire 36-37
  Standardbred 33
  Tennessee Walking
  horse 33
  Tersk 35
  Trakehner 35

Vladmir Heavy
  Draft 38
  Welsh Mountain pony 30
  Welsh pony 29
Shoulder joint 11
Show saddle 53
Show jumping 42-43
Show jumping fence 42-43
Show jumping saddle
  43, 52-53
Sidesaddle 53
Side strap 46
Silks 44-45, 59
Silver 47, 48
Silver decoration 49
Single stirrup 53
Sinus
  Respiratory and
  circulatory systems
  (side view) 21
  Skull 12
Sinus of maxillary vein 21
Skeleton 10-11
Skirt 52
Skull 12-13
Skullcap 44-45
Sleeve 45
Sliding-cheek Liverpool
  bit 48
Slope (fence) 42
Small colon 23
Small intestine 22-23
Snaffle bit
  Bits and bridles 50-51
  Racehorse and
  jockey 44
Snaffle bridle 50-51
Snaffle racing bridle 51
Snipe 8
Sock 9
Soft bristles 54-55
Spanish horse 32
Speed 44
Sperm 24
Spermatic blood
  vessel 24
Spermatic cord 24
Spermatic nerve 24
Sphenoid sinus 12
Spinal cord 12, 18-19
Spinal root of accessory
  nerve 18
Spinal vertebra 10
Spleen 23
Splenic vein 21
Splenius muscle 16-17
Splint bone 10-11
Splint boot 43
Splinter bar 47
Sponge 54-55
Sponging the eyes
  and nostrils 54-55
Spotted cap 45
Spotted sleeve 45
Spread 42
Squamous part of temporal
  bone 12
Stable cloth 55
Stainless steel bit 50
Staircase (fence) 43
Stallion 59
"Stamped" shoe 56
Stance 26
Standard (fence) 42-43
Standardbred 33, 44
Standing martingale 59
Stapes 19
Star (facial marking)
  Facial markings 8
  Head external
  features 7
Star (racing-silk
  marking) 45
Stays 47
Steel stirrup iron 52
Steeplechase 59
  Racing 44
Sternocephalicus
  muscle 17
Sternum
  Digestive system
  (side view) 22
  Skeleton 11
Stiff bristles 54-55
Stifle 59

Stifle joint
  Horse external features 6
  Racehorse and jockey 45
  Skeleton 10
Stilt 47
Stirrup
  Harness racing 44
  Saddle 52-53
Stirrup bar 52
Stirrup in run-up
  position 52
Stirrup iron 59
  Racehorse and jockey 45
  Saddles 52
  Show jumping 43
Stirrup leather
  Racehorse and jockey 45
  Saddle 52-53
Stirrup leather
  keeper 52-53
Stocking 8
Stomach 22-23
Straight bar 48
Straight-bar mouthpiece 50
Straight-bar pelham 50
Straight-cut flap 53
Strap attachment 49
Strap stay 49
Strap to crupper 49
Stripe 8
Striped jacket 45
Stud book 59
Sudadero 53
Suede seat 53
Suffolk Punch 36
Sulky 44, 59
Superficial digital flexor
  tendon 16-17
Superficial gluteal
  muscle 16
Superficial muscle 16
Superficial pectoral
  muscle 17
Superficial temporal
  artery 21
Superficial temporal vein 21
Support stake 42
Supraorbital process of
  frontal bone 13
Surcingle 59
  Racehorse and jockey 45
Surcingle loop 52
Surgical shoe 56, 59
Suspensory ligament 16-17
Suspensory ligament
  of lens 18
Sweat scraper 54-55
Swingletree 46
Sympathetic trunk 19

T

Tack 59
Tail
  Appaloosa 9
  Arabian 34
  Ariègeois pony 31
  Australian pony 30-31
  Bardigiano 28
  Camargue 9
  Cleveland Bay 9
  Color 8-9
  Connemara 9
  Dartmoor pony 29
  Exmoor pony 30
  Fell pony 30
  Foal development 26-27
  Frederiksborg 9, 32
  Friesian 9
  Grooming 54-55
  Haflinger pony 31
  Holsteiner 9
  Horse external features 6
  Icelandic horse 30
  Landais pony 31
  Lipizzaner 32
  Lusitano 9
  North Swedish horse 38
  Norwegian Fjord 28-29
  Orlov Trotter 8
  Palomino 9
  Pinto 8
  Poitevin 38
  Pottock pony 31

(Tail continued)
Racehorse and jockey 45
Rocky Mountain pony 29
Russian Heavy Draft 38
Show jumping 43
Welsh Mountain pony 30
Tail depressor muscle 16
Tarpan 58
Tarsal joint 6
Tarsals 10-11
Tassel 52-53
Team 46
Teeth **14-15**
Fetus' development 27
Temporal artery 21
Temporal bone 12
Temporal crest
Adult teeth 15
Skull (side view) 12
Temporal vein 21
Tendon
External features 6-7
Muscles 16-17
Tennessee Walking
horse 33
Tensor fascial latae
muscle 16
Tersk 35
Testis 24
Thimble 44
Thoracic vertebra 11
Thoracodorsal nerve 19
Thoroughbred 32, 44-45
Three-beat gait 40
Throat 7
Throatlatch 59
Bits and bridles 50-51
Closed bridle 48
Racehorse and jockey 44
Show jumping 43
Tibia 10-11
Tibial artery 20

Tibial muscle 16
Tibial nerve 18
Tibial vein 20
Tire
Dray harness 46
Harness racing 44
Toad eye 30
Tongs 56
Top pommel 53
Trace chain
Dray harness 47
Plow harness 46
Wagon harness 48
Traces 45
Trachea 20-21
Tracheobronchial
lymph node 20
Trakehner 35
Transverse cubital
artery 21
Transverse nasal muscle 17
Trapezius muscle 17
Tree 52
Triceps muscle 16-17
Trigeminal nerve 18-19
Trimming the hoof 56
Triple bar 42-43
Trochlear nerve 18-19
Trot 59
Gait 40-41
Tuba coxa 10
Tuber coxae 25
Tuber sacrale 25
Tug 48
Tunica albuginea of corpus
cavernosum 24
Turbinate bone 12
Two-beat gait 40
Two-wheeled cart 44
Tympanic cavity 19
Tympanic membrane 19
Type 6, 59

U

Ulna 11
Ulnar artery 21
Ulnar carpal flexor
muscle 17
Ulnar nerve 19
Ulnar vein 21
Umbilical cord 26
Unclipped area 54
Unerupted adult
premolar 14
Upper canine 13
Upper eyelid 18
Upper incisor 12-13
Upper jaw
Skull 12
Teeth 14-15
Upper lip 7
Upper molar 13
Upper premolar 13
Upright 42
Upright planks 42-43
Upright poles 42-43
Ureter 24-25
Urethra 24-25
Urethral muscle 25
Urethral orifice 24
Urinary system 24
Urinogenital system
24-25
Using the dandy brush 55
Uterus
Fetus' development 26-27
Urinogenital system 24-25

V

Vagina 25
Vagus nerve 18-19

Vascular impression of
mandible 12-13
Vas deferens 24-25
Vein
Circulatory system 20-21
Liver 23
Muscles (side view) 17
Urinary system 24
Vena cava
Circulatory system 20-21
Liver 23
Urinary system 24
Venous plexus 20-21
Venous sinus 21
Ventral band 23
Ventral nasal meatus 12
Ventral part of colon 23
Ventral serratus muscle 17
Ventral turbinate bone 12
Ventricle 20-21
Ventricular septum 20
Vertebra
Digestive system
(side view) 23
Skeleton 10-11
Skull 12
Urinogenital system
24-25
Vertebral artery 21
Vertebral vein 21
Vertical ramus of
mandible 12
Vesicular gland 24-25
Vestibule (ear) 19
Vestibule (urinogenital
system) 25
Vitreous humor 18
Vladmir Heavy Draft 38
Voluntary muscle 16, 18
Vulcanite-covered
mouthpiece 50
Vulva 25

W

Wagon 46, 48
Wagon harness 48
Waist 52
Walk 59
Gait 40-41
Wall 42-43
War horses 36
Washing the horse 54
Water brush 55
Water jump 42
Weaning 26
Web schooling rein 51
Welsh Mountain
pony 30
Welsh pony 29
Western bridle 50-51
Western saddle 52-53
Wheel
Harness racing 44
Plow 47
Wagon harness 48
Whip 44-45
White face 8
Width 42
Wild ass 58
Wild horse 6, 8, 58
Wing of atlas 7
Withers 59
American Shetland
pony 28
Anglo-Arab 34
Arabian 34
Australian pony 30-31
Bashkir 29
Boulonnais 37
Budonny 35
Caspian pony 31
Clydesdale 36
Dales pony 29

Dartmoor pony 29
External features 6-7
Foal development 26
Frederiksborg 32
Hanoverian 32-33
Landais pony 31
Morgan 33
New Forest pony 28
Norwegian Fjord
28-29
Nonius 35
Pottock pony 31
Quarter horse 33
Rocky Mountain
pony 29
Saddlebred 33
Selle Français 35
Shire 36-37
Standardbred 33
Suffolk Punch 36
Tennessee Walking
horse 33
Trakehner 35
Wooden blocks (fence) 43

XYZ

Yearling 59
Zebra 58
Zebroid 59
Hybrid 58
Zedonk 59
Hybrid 58
Zygomatic arch
Skeleton (side view) 11
Skull (side view) 13
Zygomatic bone 13
Zygomatic process
Adult teeth 15
Skull (side view) 12
Zygomatic ridge 13

Acknowledgments

Dorling Kindersley would like to thank:
Brian Crane AFCL Farrier, New Barnet, Hertfordshire, UK;
the Whitbread Hop Farm, Paddock Wood, Kent, UK; James
Fanshawe; the Royal Veterinary College, London, UK; Jockey
Club Estates Limited, UK; the National Shire Horse Centre,
Plymouth, Devon, UK; W. H. Gidden Ltd., London, UK; the
Marwell Zoological Park, Winchester, Hampshire, UK;
Pauline Jones and Jaffa, owned by Mrs. Bonner

Picture credits:
2c, 6cl Thoroughbred - *Lyphento*, Conkwell Grange Stud,
Avon, UK; 8bl Orlov Trotter - Moscow Hippodrome, Russian
Federation; 8br, 8cr Pinto - *Hit Man*, Boyd Cantrell, Kentucky
Horse Park, US; 2cr and 8cl Gelderlander - *Spooks*, Peter
Munt, Ascot Driving Stables, Berkshire, UK; 6-7main, 7br, 8tc
Danish Warmblood - *Rambo*, Jorgen Olsen, Denmark; 9tl
Connemara - *Spinway Bright Morning*, Miss S. Hodgkins,
Spinway Stud, Oxfordshire, UK; 9tc, 4l Lusitano -
Montemere-O-Nova, Nan Thurman, Turville Valley Stud,
Oxfordshire, UK; 9cl Palomino - *Wychwood Dynascha*, Mrs.
G. Harwood, Wychwood Stud, Gloucestershire, UK; 9cr
Friesian - *Sjouke*, Sonia Gray, Tattondale Carriages,
Cheshire, UK; 9cl Camargue - *Redounet*, Mr. Contreras, Les
Saintes Maries de la Mer, France; 9bl Holsteiner - *Lenard*,
Sue Watson, Trenawin Stud, Cornwall, UK; 9br Appaloosa -
Golden Nugget, Sally Chaplin; 28tl Falabella - *Pegasus of
Kilverstone*, Lady Fisher, Kilverstone Wildlife Park, Norfolk,
UK; 28bl New Forest pony - *Bowerwood Aquila*, Mrs. Rae
Turner, Bowerwood Stud, Hampshire, UK; 28tr American
Shetland pony - *Little Trouble*, Marvin McCabe, Kentucky
Horse Park, US; 28cr Bardigiano - *Pippo*, Istituto Incremento
Ippico di Crema, Italy; 28-29b Norwegian Fjord - *Ausdan
Svejk*, John Goddard Fenwick and Lyn Moran, Ausdan Stud,
Dyfed, UK; 29tl Rocky Mountain pony - *Mocha Monday*, Rea
Swan, Hope Springs Farm, Kentucky Horse Park, US; 29tc
Welsh pony - *Twyford Signal*, Mr. and Mrs. L. E. Bigley,
Llanarth Stud, Hereford, UK; 29tr, 8tl Highland pony - *Fruich
of Dykes*, Countess of Swinton, UK; 29cl Bashkir - *Mel's Lucky
Boy*, Dan Stewart Family, Kentucky Horse Park, US; 29c
Dales pony - *Warrenlane Duke*, Mr. Dickson, Millbeck Pony
Stud, Yorkshire, UK; 29br, 4r Dartmoor pony - *Allendale
Vampire*, Miss M. Houlden, Haven Stud, Hereford, UK; 30tl
Icelandic pony - *Leiknir*, Kentucky Horse Farm, US; 30cl, 6tl
Exmoor pony - *Murrayton Delphinus*, June Freeman,
Murrayton Stud, Hertfordshire, UK; 30bl Fell pony -
Waverhead William, Mr. and Mrs. S. Errington, UK; 30br
Welsh Mountain pony - *Bengad Dark Mullein*, Mrs. C.

Bowyer, Symondsbury Stud, Sussex, UK; 30-31main
Australian pony - *Malibu Park Command Performance*,
K. and L. Sinclair, Victoria, Australia; 31tl Caspian pony -
Hopstone Shabdiz, Mrs. Scott, Henden Caspian Stud,
Wiltshire, UK; 31tr Haflinger pony - *Nomad*, Miss Helen
Blair, Silvretta Haflinger Stud, West Midlands, UK; 31cr
Pottock pony - *Thouarec III*, Haras National de Tarbes,
France; 31cl Ariègeois pony - *Radium*, Haras National de Pau,
France; 31bl Hackney pony - *Hurstwood Consort*, Mr. and
Mrs. Hayden, Hurstwood Stud, UK; 31br, 8cr Landais pony -
Hippolyte, Haras National de Pau, France; 32bl, 9bc
Frederiksborg - *Zarif Langløkkegard*, Harry Nielsen,
Denmark; 32cr, 9tr Cleveland Bay - *Oaten Mainbrace*, Mr.
and Mrs. Dimmock; 32br Lipizzaner - *Siglavy Szella*, John
Goddard Fenwick and Lyn Moran; 32-33main Hanoverian -
Défilante, Barry Mawdsley, European Horse Enterprises,
Berkshire, UK; 33tl Tennessee Walking horse - *Delight's
Moondust*, Andrew and Jane Shaw, Kentucky Horse Park,
US; 33tc Morgan - *Fox Creek's Dynasty*, Darwin Olsen,
Kentucky Horse Park, US; 33tr Saddlebred - *Kinda Kostly*,
Kentucky Horse Park, US; 33cr, 2tr, 8tr Quarter horse - *Doc's
Maharajah*, Harold Bush, Kentucky Horse Park, US; 33br
Standardbred - *Rambling Willie*, Farrington Stables and
Estate of Paul Siebert, Kentucky Horse Park, US; 34tl Arabian
- *Muskhari Silver*, Janet and Anne Connolly, Silver Fox
Arabians, West Midlands, UK; 34tr Akhal-Teke - *Fakir-Bola*,
Moscow Hippodrome, Russian Federation; 34cr Kabardin -
Moscow Hippodrome, Russian Federation; 34br Barb - *Taw's
Little Buck*, Kentucky Horse Park, US; 2bl and 34cl Shagya
Arabian - *Artaxerxes*, Jeanette Bauch and Jens Brinksten,
Denmark; 34bl and 4r Anglo-Arab - *Restif*, Haras National De
Compiègne, France; 35tl Don - *Baret*, Moscow Hippodrome,
Russian Federation; 35tc Trakehner - *Muschamp Mauersee*,
Janet Lorch, Muschamp Stud, Buckinghamshire, UK; 35tr
Budonny - *Barin*, Moscow Hippodrome, Russian Federation;
35c Nonius - *Pampas*, A. G. Kishumseigi, Hungary; 2cr, 8cl,
35cr Dutch Warmblood - *Edison*, Mrs. Dejonge; 35cl French
Trotter - *Pur Historien*, Haras National de Compiègne,
France; 35bl Selle Français - *Prince D'elle*, Haras Natonal De
Saint Lô, France; 35br, 5cl Andalusian - *Campanero XXIV*,
Nigel Oliver, Singleborough Stud, Buckinghamshire, UK;
36tl, 54tl Suffolk Punch - *Laurel Keepsake II*, P. Adams and
Sons; 36bl Clydesdale - *Blue Print*, Mervyn and Pauline
Ramage, Mount Farm, Clydesdale horses, Tyne and Wear,
UK; 36-37main Shire - *Duke*, Jim Lockwood, Courage Shire
Horse Centre, Buckinghamshire, UK; 37tr, 4c Breton -

Ulysses, Haras National de Tarbes, France; 37cr Boulonnais -
Urus, Haras National de Compiègne, France; 37cr Norman
Cob - *Ibis*, Haras National de Compiègne, France; 37cl Brabant -
Roy, Kentucky Horse Park, US; 37br Jutland - *Tempo*, Jørgen
Neilsen, Denmark; 37bl Italian Heavy Draft - *Nobile*, Istituto
Incremento Ippico di Crema, Italy; 38tl Russian Heavy Draft -
Bespechny, Moscow Agricultural Academy, Russian
Federation; 38cl Vladmir Heavy Draft - *Vostorg*, Central
Moscow Hippodrome, Russian Federation; 38c Murakozer -
Baba, Kobza Istvan; 38cr North Swedish horse - *Ysterman*,
Ingvar Andersson, Sweden; 38bl Dutch Draft - *Marquis van
de Lindenhoeve*, Albert ter wal; 38bc Comtois - *Attila*, Haras
de Pau, France; 38br Poitevin - *Vitrisse*, Haras National de la
Roche sur yon, France; 6bl, 38-39main Percheron - *Tango*,
Haras National de Saint Lô, France; 39tr, 9c, 4l Ardennais -
Ramses du Vallon, Haras National de Pau, France; 58tl Riding
pony - *Brutt*, Robert Oliver

Photography:
Dave King 1; Steve Gorton 5br, 52br, 53r; Andy Crawford 3c,
46tr, 47t, 48-49; Dave Rudkin 2tc, 2br, 5tl, 44, 45main, 45tr,
51r, 52tr; Tim Ridley 12, 13main, 13tr, 50r, 51tl, 51tc, 53tl,
53cl, 53bl; Colin Keates of the Natural History Museum 10,
11main, 14bl, 14br, 15bl, 15br; Gordon Clayton 5tr, 26bl,
26bc, 26br, 27bl, 27br; Jerry Young 26tl, 43b, 44b, 52tl, 56tl,
56bl, 56br, 56cr, 56-57main, 57br, 57cr, 58tr, 58br, 58cl,
58bl, 58bcl; Bob Langrish 5cr, 40-41main, 42tl; Karl Shone
46-47main, 51cl; Bruce Coleman Limited/Jane Burton 27tr;
Anna Hodgson 56tr, 57t; Peter Chadwick 50tl, 51bl, 52bl,
54bl, 54bc, 54-55main, 55cl, 55bl, 55cr, 55br; Stephen Oliver
8br, 50l

(t=top, b=bottom, l=left, r=right, c=center)

Picture research:
Joanna Thomas

Additional illustrations:
Roy Flooks; Selwyn Hutchinson; Simone End; John
Temperton; Sandra Pond and Will Giles

Additional editorial assistance:
Geoffrey Stalker; Liz Wheeler

Index:
Susan Bosanko